# Another Way to Dance

# Another Way to Dance

Contemporary Asian Poetry from Canada and the United States

*edited by*

Cyril Dabydeen

TSAR
Toronto
Oxford
1996

The publishers acknowledge generous assistance
from the Ontario Arts Council and the Canada Council.

Cover art by Aries Cheung.

**Canadian Cataloguing in Publication Data**

Main entry under title:

Another way to dance : contemporary Asian poetry from
    Canada and the United States

ISBN 0-920661-59-9

1. Canadian poetry (English) - Asian-Canadian authors.*
2. Canadian poetry (English) - 20th century.
3. American poetry - Asian American authors.
4. American poetry - 20th century.    I. Dabydeen, Cyril, 1945-

PS8283.A8A67  1996      C811'.5408'0895071      C96-932361-1
PR9195.35.A8A67  1996

TSAR Publications
P.O. Box 6996, Station A
Toronto, M5W 1X7  Canada

# Contents

# Contents

Contents

*ix*

# Introduction

## I.

The idea of putting together this anthology of poets of Asian background living in Canada and the United States came to me upon realizing the continuing interest expressed in its previous, more limited, manifestation, *Another Way to Dance: Asian Canadian Poets* (Williams-Wallace, 1990), now out of print. I kept being aware of the many possibilities and sensibilities at work associated with the temperament of place and the varying voices, sometimes changing and reorganizing the way we view the world. This perhaps is inevitable in the context of the power of language and imagery evoked in the quest to make our lives significant—as we continue to shape our identities in becoming who we truly are. And, indeed, in this collection are poems of personal truths, personal testimonies: perhaps if only reflecting one editor's fascination with poetry; this in the context of the many distinctive voices grappling with bold or strikingly new visions in the flux of time and change in North America. Yet, regardless of age or experience, the poets represented here are often loyal to their disparate Asian roots and ancestry in adding to the richness of the literature and cultural life around them, reflected in their expanding range, points of view and consciousness, informed by an ever powerful memory and myth in creating new poetry.

The semantics associated with the terms "Asian-American" and "Asian-Canadian" are sometimes elusive, not easy to define or categorize, yet are relevant in the demographic flux alluded to above; and generic as they are, they are particular in their references to a loose association of countries in Southeast and Southern Asia. Underlying this is the discourse relating to diaspora, especially for those Asians (like myself) who, generations later, might have found themselves in apparently non-Asian parts of the world, such as Africa or the Caribbean; but all are trying to wrest an identity of interconnectedness in the unfolding mythology and environment of the new place—whether seen as the ongoing frontier associated with the landscape of the imagination, or merely metaphorically as the "Great White North."

The poets in this anthology, living and working in North America, are continually coming to grips with manifold sensibilities fashioned by an unpredictable destiny in the struggle to adapt, while simultaneously pursuing art and their individual selves: conjuring up memories, hurts, passions, new longings, changing and being changed by the spirit of the place. The inevitable challenge in this cultural evolution is in trying to maintain integrity of the poetic voice: to be what we truly are without necessarily clinging to ancient allegiances, save for that which is deep within, even if akin to "a thousand suns," as New York-based Indian-born poet Meena Alexander says. As individual suns glitter, coruscate, there is also at the formal level the conviction that the traditional literary canon is no longer the imperative, for in the choreography of change and evolution there is and always will be—*another way to dance*.

## II.

Sometime from about the mid-seventies to the eighties, I became associated, serendipitously, with organizing readings of writers under the auspices of the Canadian Asian Studies Association (a Learned Society) from Halifax to Vancouver in the Association's assemblies across the country: this task came about initially at the urging of the Japanese-Canadian poet and novelist Joy Kogawa. Over those years she inspired me to continue with this effort as I interacted with other poets and writers of diverse Asian backgrounds, including the late Reshard Gool and, in different circumstances, with the more widely known Michael Ondaatje (through my membership of the League of Canadian Poets). The sense of developing a community of creative like-minded souls grew stronger within me in an increasingly changing North American world of ideas and art as demographics and the "shifting ground" of place continued to influence our lives. I also became conversant with the aspirations of members of the Asian Canadian Writers Workshop, both in Vancouver and Toronto, all imbued with a strong sense of their particular roots and identities. Subsequently, in the early eighties I undertook a study entitled "Asian Canadian Writers: A Bio-Bibliographic Survey and Profile" (with federal government support), perhaps a seminal exercise because it preceded other works, for instance *A Meeting of Streams* (TSAR, 1985), a collection of surveys and studies on South Asian writers in Canada. At this time, new Asian-American anthologies were in the works, the most notable being Joseph Bruhac's edition of *Breaking Silence: An Anthology of Asian-American Poetry* (Greenfield Review Press, 1984). In the latter, Joy Kogawa and I are the only Canadians included; and, reading this anthology many times over (because it is one of the finest with distinct energies), I became more conscious of the distinctive poetic voice among the range of writers with Asian roots, including those in *Paper Doors: An Anthology of Japanese-Canadian Poetry* (Coach House Press, 1981). I also kept comparing the achievements of those writers south of the Canadian border, with others, while reflecting on the many poets' verve, passion and skill: poets such as Arthur Sze, David Mura, Marilyn Chin, Mei-Mei Berssenbrugge, Garrett Hongo, Cathy Song, Kimiko Hahn, all included in this anthology, and others such as Lawson Faluda.

The more I read and became acquainted with the range of American and Canadian talents, the more I began to hear it being said that the regular mainstream anthologies tended not to reflect the true diversity around them, partly due to the fact that their editors would not be fully aware of the extent of the changes taking place and the creative energies in communities other than those they were most familiar with. It is for this reason that I embarked on editing *A Shapely Fire: Changing the Literary Landscape* (Mosaic Press, 1987) to broaden the reader's perspective. With new challenges appearing, the so-called other is now becoming more apparent and palpable in the discourse and dialectic of place and ethnicity juxtaposed with an ongoing wrestle with nationalism, as literature continues to evolve on both sides of the border. In this context, I am beginning to reflect on a continental view of diversity and multiculturalism, as opposed to the limitation of a garrison mentality respecting cultural achievement, as I have heard mentioned in the Canadian context.

Poetry, and literature as a whole, indeed can never truly be suppressed; for we have heard of breaking silences, the assertion of will through strength and power of the imagination: the sheer numinous echoes of art and intuition will always prevail, as all the writers in this collection no doubt believe. In creating their literature, personal mythologies of moments of transfiguration often seem all, transcending concrete political-cum-historical acts such as the internment of the Japanese-Americans and Japanese-Canadians during the Second World War, the head tax imposed on the Chinese at the turn of the century, or the conviction of the legacy of farm and railway labour experience; or, even the alienation felt by many stemming from discriminatory treatment and exclusion. In all this, language continues to play a key role in determining how we view history and ourselves, as we seek ways of reacting to and reshaping the historical past without necessarily being silenced. And poetry will continue to play a role in helping to reconstruct or reshape the imagination and consciousness; in asserting a strong voice we will keep defining the sense of who we truly are in striving to achieve personal exaltation and simultaneously finding acceptance and fulfilment.

## III.

In my own readings across Canada, I have sometimes shared the stage with many of the Canadian poets in this collection; I have also shared strong friendships with poets like Rienzi Crusz, Joy Kogawa, and Lakshmi Gill, in the process of becoming or in simply being. The Asian-Americans I feel I have now come to know better as a consequence of working on this anthology: many of them I previously read only in the small literary magazines and sometimes in book form, such as David Mura and Meena Alexander; and other American poets like Arthur Sze, Mei-Mei Berssenbrugge, and Agha Shahid Ali I have talked with on the phone as I became fully absorbed in the work of preparing this anthology. David Mura's comments about the anthology being a "gift to our communities" is touching; and Arthur Sze's, Marilyn Chin's, Chitra Divakaruni's, and Cathy Song's quick responses to my invitation to submit their poetry convinced me of a sense of a shared spirit and generosity at work, as well as a vital community presence despite artificial borders sometimes extending from Hawaii and across the United States to various parts of Canada, as we wrestle with our double or sometimes triple identities, but always with our numinous and individual selves intact—being artists first of all.

Michael Ondaatje, now a Canadian "institution," has long said that you adapt the country in which you live; this is apt in view of the fact that in *Another Way to Dance* are some of the bold new metaphors of place, work, family, climate, and sometimes the longing for another place and time, but always with a new affirmation, expressed with passion, humour, wit, even a biting irony while exulting in images of a positive striving to share fully in the North American experience. In the creative act, all the anxieties become dualities and are transformed in the oneness of the personal voice, or the silent clamour of the spirit. Images of belonging converge and become evocative, or are simply carved eloquently in a laconic silence: as in Joy Kogawa's poetry, or in Gerry Shikatani's and Cathy Song's unique rhythms. Herein, too, lie the resonances of a genuine poetic identity; and one can say that the poems included in this anthology are the stories of validation: all collectively participate in defining place and time in the drama of solid, palpable emotions of heart and soul, mind and spirit within identifiable Asian roots and ancestry—if only conveyed as "the portable home of the imagination," as has been said.

The assertion of spirit and self and family in poets as disparate as Rienzi Crusz (Ontario) and Wing Tek Lum (Hawaii); or in Uma Parameswaran (Manitoba), Surjeet Kalsey (British Columbia) and Bhargavi

Mandava (California) asserting woman's particular reality—combine with other delicate feelings reflected in the directness of the voice in, for instance, Jim Wong-Chu, Kevin Irie, and Nguyen Chi Thien responding to social situations and inheritances. These feelings juxtapose with the unique subtleties and energies of other poetry, by S Padmanab, Mina Kumar, and Kimiko Hahn. Particular echoes in Sally Ito, Sadhu Binning, and Suwanda Sugunasiri sometimes match the verbal and structural experimentation seen in Rita Wong, Carolyn Lau-lanilau, and Garrett Hongo, as all combine the sense of language in realizing obvious or arcane truths. In Suniti Namjoshi, the sometimes fabulist rendering of a place and time is resonant, whether it be only that of the quest for home and other longings; this latter is also seen in the personal but bold associations of Himani Bannerji, Lakshmi Gill, Krisantha Sri Bhaggiyadatta, and Ian Iqbal Rashid, or the delicate lines of May Seung Jew and Carol Roh-Spaulding. Metaphorical expressions of Caribbean sensibilities in Ramabai Espinet, Madeline Coopsammy, and Sasenarine Persaud contrast interestingly with the delicate execution of lines by Arthur Sze and Mei-mei Berssenbrugge, whose verbal tapestries are a continuing delight. Yet the overall authenticity in all the poets rings true, for nothing in their individual selves or in their intimate intuitions is straightforward or linear; nothing also is overextended or overblown; the energy of resonances is all, as, for instance, in Agha Shahid Ali's command of his metaphors. And confidence of technique and verbal presence combine in chiselled execution seen powerfully in David Mura's poems. Socially aware depictions of a former homeland are also reflected with a sense of iconoclasm mixed with tradition in the poems by Krisantha Sri Bhaggiyadatta and Asoka Weerasinghe reinforcing their Sri Lankan roots, confirming that memory is indeed "the mother of the muses." Similarly, Marilyn Chin's, Bhargavi Mandava's, Kimiko Hahn's and Marilyn Chin's renditions hold strong: an unerring ear for the colloquial juxtaposed with controlled rhythms seems all as everything throbs at the moment of full realization.

## IV.

If the apparent homogeneity expressed in the term "Asian" stems from the function of ethnicity, it merely alludes to an illusory uniformity responding to the immediate and particular world around; and my own poems sometimes reflect the desire to intermingle and integrate the personal with the present landscape in concrete ways, believing as I do with all other writers, that coming to grips with real experiences can only be realized in innate, personal ways, even as we grapple with social concerns and spiritual longings, using models that might have been acquired elsewhere. In Ondaatje's unique poetic prism, for instance, powerful ironies are always fashioned by his unique verbal flexibility. And, significantly, all the writers in this anthology have brought their experiences to bear in identifiable or distinct ways in the context of the facility of the English language itself: reflected markedly in David Mura's biting assertions in "Caliban" or in Chitra Divakaruni's double-edged "Making Samosas." Thus, in these poems language-use gives a definite sense of the rhythms of a particular voice as the writers embrace the challenge of being both Asian and North American, while simultaneously seeking to resolve the dilemma of a divided identity through continuing to evoke memory. Overall, the vision compels the poet to see, often in one clear glance, as reflected in the striving for the perfect line by an accomplished poet such as Rienzi Crusz; or in the other poets, who may be as far afield as second- or third-generation Canadians like Kevin Irie, Gerry Shikatani, and Joy Kogawa.

Putting this anthology together has meant being more crucially aware, also, of nuances relating to gender and geography. And what is remarkable is that all the poets agreed to share their personal selves with readers towards a collective sensibility and poignancy. It is also important to add that other talented poets such as Evelyn Lau or Roy Miki could have easily been included here, but for their different priorities at the time of my invitation to them to contribute. And, in this collection, I admit that it has been a deliberate effort to give the Canadian poets more space, bearing in mind the anthologies already in existence with American concentration; as well as the fact that many of the Asian-American poets have expressed the desire to find out more about the work of their Canadian counterparts in the overall sharing that is taking place.

Because anthologies are never-ending, never complete in themselves, *Another Way to Dance* is simply meant for the reader to experience some of the rhythms in poetry written by a particular group; and no doubt to encourage the reader to seek out these and other writers of Asian background more fully, as well as those of other ethnicities or common background, in the ongoing evolution and the seeking after aesthetic satisfaction.

I express thanks to M G Vassanji for his pioneer activity with *The Toronto South Asian Review,* and to Nurjehan Aziz of TSAR Publications for agreeing to publish this book because of its value to "communities": some of the works included here were originally published by TSAR; to American poets Arthur Sze, Marilyn Chin, David Mura, Cathy Song: for the genuine warmth of spirit and enthusiasm; for Joy Kogawa's original inspiration; the warm support of poets like Rienzi Crusz and Madeline Coopsammy,

*Introduction*

and the other Canadian writers who might not be distinctly Asian (like the Jewish-Canadian poet Seymour Mayne); to poet Joseph Bruhac—a Native American—for his immediate assistance to get the American side of this collection going, as well as for his seminal anthologizing with *Breaking Silence;* and to Peter Nazareth (University of Iowa International Writing Program). Thanks also to the editors of other anthologies such as *Paper Doors, Open Boat,* and *Geography of Voice,* and *Voices: Canadian Writers of African Descent,* as well as to those of more "mainstream" anthologies which I continually read—all engaged in acts of collecting and fashioning selves, with the belief foremost in the intrinsic value of poetry. Significant, also, is the fact that an anthology is primarily an effort aimed at providing pleasures in reading it, while inspiring confidence to seek out the poets' individual works towards finding a glimmer of illumination of one's own self while grappling with the spirit of communities elsewhere.

Cyril Dabydeen
November 1996

# Meena Alexander

## BROWN SKIN WHAT MASK?

Babel's township seeps into Central Park
I hunch on a stone bench scraping nightingale-bulbuls
cuckoo-koels, rose-gulabs off my face

No flim-flam now; cardsharp, streetwise
I fix my heels at Paul's Shoe Place for a dollar fifty
get a free makeover at Macy's, eyes smart, lips shine.
Shall I be a hyphenated thing, Macaulay's Minutes
and Melting Pot theories notwithstanding?

Shall I bruise my skin, burn up into
She Who Is No Color whose longing is a crush
of larks shivering without sound?

When lit by his touch in a public place
—an elevator with a metal face—shall I finger grief for luck
work stares into the "bride is never naked" stuff?

# PASSION

I.

After childbirth
the tenth month's passion:

a bloodiness
still shifting at her core
she crawls on the mud floor

past the empty rice sacks
blown large with dust,
rims distended like sails.

Her skin scrapes a tin bowl
with water from the stream,
a metal frame

bearing a god
whose black blue face
melts into darkness, as a gem might

tossed back
into its own
implacable element.

She waits,
she sets her sari to her teeth
and when the chattering begins

fierce, inhuman joy,
monkeys rattling the jamun tree,
bellies distended, washed with wind

she screams
and screams
a raw, ungoverned thing.

II.

There are beetles scrabbling
in the open sacks,
chaff flies in the half light
a savage sound in her eyes
struck free

the human realms of do and don't
the seemingly precise, unalterable keys
dashed to a frenzy
and still the voice holds.

III.

One summer' s day
I saw a heron
small and grey
blinded by an eagle's claw

it dashed its head
against the Coromandel rock.

The bleeding head
hung on
by a sinew or two

as the maimed bird
struck
and struck again

then turned to rise
an instant
on its sunlit wings.

It was carved in bronze
against the crawling foam

agony
the dead cannot know
in their unaltered kingdoms.


IV.

I am she
the woman after giving birth

life
to give life
torn and hovering

as bloodied fluids
baste the weakened flesh.

For her
there are no words,
no bronze, no summoning.

I am her sight
her hearing
and her tongue.

I am she
smeared with ash
from the black god's altar

I am
the sting of love
the blood hot flute
the face
carved in the window,
watching as the god set sail
across the waters
risen from the Cape,
Sri Krishna in a painted catamaran.

I am she
tongueless in rhapsody

the stars of glass
nailed to the Southern sky.

Ai ai

she cried.

They stuffed
her mouth with rags

and pulled her
from the wooden bed
and thrust her
to the broken floor.

I, I.

# ELEPHANTS IN HEAT

Soon after we met
you sent me a book
it had many pictures of elephants

I saw a male beast
scorched by stove fire
belly and curling tail stacked
with precise flesh
eyes irregular in passion.

On the margins faced in red,
two others sporting,

a female down below
licked by waterlilies,
buoyant in the curlicues of waves.

I used to make up nightmares as a child
so mother would come in
and lift me up, lips wet
in all that moonlight.

I saw elephants in heat
crawl over garden trees
the myena's nest slipped loose,
it clung to ivory

The sky was colored in blood
as in this painting
*Elephant on a Summer Day*
Bundi School, circa 1750.

I wonder what it knew
that painter's eye
seared by a fullness we cannot seize
in stanzas stone or canvas
short of stark loss

Our wiry bounding lines
silks and weathered ivories
scored by the Kerala sun

Thinned and dissolved
into desire's rondures
mad covenant of flesh

A beast unpacking
delight from his trunk
your tongue scorching mine
undercover this spring season

As sulphur bubbles from limestone

and the unquiet heart
like the pale monkey in the painting
takes it all in.


# NEWS OF THE WORLD

We must always return
to poems for news of the world
or perish for the lack

Strip it
block it with blood
the page is not enough
unless the sun rises in it.

Old doctor Willi writes
crouched on a stoop
in Paterson, New Jersey.

I am torn by light

She cries into her own head.
The playing fields of death
are far from me. In Cambodia I carried
my mother's head in a sack
and ran three days and nights
through a rice field

Now I pick up vegetables
from old sacking and straighten
them on crates: tomatoes
burning plums, cabbages hard
as bone. I work in Manhattan.

The subway corrupts me
with scents the robed Muslims sell

with white magazines
with spittle and gum

I get lost underground

By Yankee Stadium
I stumble out
hands loaded down
fists clenched into balls

A man approaches
muck on his shirt
his head, a battering ram
he knows who I am

I stall:
the tracks flash
with a thousand suns.


## ART OF PARIAHS

Back against the kitchen stove
Draupadi sings:

In my head Beirut still burns

The Queen of Nubia, of God's Upper Kingdom
the Rani of Jhansi, transfigured, raising her sword
are players too. They have entered with me
into North America and share these walls.

We make up an art of pariahs:

Two black children spray painted white
their eyes burning,
a white child raped in a car

for her pale skin's sake,
an Indian child stoned by a bus shelter,
they thought her white in twilight.

Someone is knocking and knocking
but Draupadi will not let him in.
She squats by the stove and sings:

The Rani shall not sheathe her sword
nor Nubia's queen restrain her elephants
till tongues of fire wrap a tender blue,
a second skin, a solace to our children

Come walk with me towards a broken wall
—Beirut still burns—carved into its face.
Outcastes all let's conjure honey scraped from stones,
an underground railroad stacked with rainbow skin,
Manhattan's mixed rivers rising.

# Agha Shahid Ali

## THE DACCA GAUZES

. . . for a whole year he sought
to accumulate the most exquisite
Dacca gauzes.
                    OSCAR WILDE, *The Picture of Dorian Gray*

Those transparent Dacca gauzes
known as woven air, running
water, evening dew:

a dead art now, dead over
a hundred years. "No one
now knows," my grandmother says,

"what it was to wear
or touch that cloth." She wore
it once, an heirloom sari from

her mother's dowry, proved
genuine when it was pulled, all
six yards, through a ring.

Years later when it tore,
many handkerchiefs embroidered
with gold-thread paisleys
were distributed among
the nieces and daughters-in-law.
Those too now lost.

In history we learned: the hands

of weavers were amputated,
the looms of Bengal silenced,

and the cotton shipped raw
by the British to England.
History of little use to her,

my grandmother just says
how the muslins of today
seem so coarse and that only

in autumn, should one wake up
at dawn to pray, can one
feel that same texture again.

One morning, she says, the air
was dew-starched: she pulled
it absently through her ring.

## A DREAM OF GLASS BANGLES

Those autumns my parents slept
warm in a quilt studded
with pieces of mirrors

On my mother's arms were bangles
like waves of frozen rivers
and at night

after the prayers
as she went down to her room
I heard the faint sound of ice

breaking on the staircase
breaking years later
into winter

our house surrounded by men
pulling icicles for torches
off the roofs

rubbing them on the walls
till the cement's darkening red
set the tips of water on fire

the air a quicksand of snow
as my father stepped out
and my mother

inside the burning house
a widow smashing the rivers
on her arms


## SNOWMEN

My ancestor, a man
of Himalayan snow,
came to Kashmir from Samarkand,
carrying a bag
of whale bones:
heirlooms from sea-funerals.
His skeleton
carved from glaciers, his breath
arctic,
he froze women in his embrace.
His wife thawed into stony water,
her old age a clear
evaporation.

This heirloom,
his skeleton under my skin, passed
from son to grandson,
generations of snowmen on my back.

They tap every year on my window,
their voices hushed to ice.

No, they won't let me out of winter,
and I've promised myself,
even if I'm the last snowman,
that I'll ride into spring
on their melting shoulders.

# I SEE KASHMIR FROM NEW DELHI AT MIDNIGHT

1.
One must wear jewelled ice in dry plains
to will the distant mountains to glass.
The city from where no news can come
is now so visible in its curfewed night
that the worst is precise:

           From Zero Bridge
a shadow chased by searchlights is running
away to find its body. On the edge
of the Cantonment, where Gupkar Road ends,
it shrivels, shrinks almost into nothing,

is nothing by Interrogation gates
so it can slip, unseen, into the cells:
Drippings from a suspended burning tire
are falling on the back of a prisoner,
the naked boy screaming, "I know nothing."

2.
The shadow slips out, beckons Console Me,
and somehow there, across five hundred miles,
I'm sheened in moonlight, in emptied Srinagar,
but without any assurance for him.

On Residency Road, by Mir Pan House,
unheard we speak: "I know those words by heart
(you once said them by chance): In autumn
when the wind blows sheer ice, the chinar leaves
fall in clusters—

                one by one, otherwise."
"Rizwan, it's you, Rizwan, it's you," I cry out
as he steps closer, the sleeves of his phiren torn.
"Each night put Kashmir in your dreams," he says,
then touches me, his hands crusted with snow,
whispers, "I have been cold a long, long time."


3.
"Don't tell my father I have died," he says,
and I follow him through blood on the road
and hundreds of pairs of shoes the mourners
left behind, as they ran from the funeral,
victims of the firing. From windows we hear
grieving mothers, and snow begins to fall
on us, like ash. Black on edges of flames,
it cannot extinguish the neighborhoods,
the homes set ablaze by midnight soldiers.
Kashmir is burning:

                By that dazzling light
we see men removing statues from temples.
We beg them, "Who'll protect us if you leave?"
They don't answer, just keep disappearing
on the road to the plains, clutching the gods.


4.
I won't tell your father you've died, Rizwan,
but where has your shadow fallen, like cloth
on the tomb of which saint, or the body
of which unburied boy in the mountains,
bullet-torn, like you, his blood sheer rubies

14

on Himalayan snow?

                I've tied a knot
with green thread at Shah Hamdan, to be
untied only when the atrocities
are stunned by your jewelled return, but no news
escapes the curfew, nothing of your shadow,
and I'm back, five hundred miles, taking off
my ice, the mountains granite again as I see
men coming from those Abodes of Snow
with gods asleep like children in their arms.

# *Himani Bannerji*

## VOYAGE

poised
you are afraid

the night crumbles into dust
and wind rustles
under the window ledge
and trees in the backyard
of an unknown house
shake down their last leaves

the house sets sails
into the night
into the unknown seas
and the voyage begins

and poised
you are afraid
reinventing yourself
in these high seas, strange lands
where an occasional hieroglyph
signals recognition
the eye perhaps or the bird
or that simple talon of a hook

what now? who will hear you?
who knows you there or here on this ship
where we pace the deck?
why on rainy afternoons of wet
dark greens and the bruised berries

of red, the knitted shawl and small
pillows, tea and talk later, you murmur
a litany—"not enough, not enough, not . . ."

So the wind, the ship
in the dark edge of the night
and fear, such young dark fears
who weep words, meanings
and extend a hand
a letter perhaps
in the high dark seas
as we move to a land nameless
where no self, no you, no mail
by land or sea have been invented
where I voyage alone
poised and afraid.

(April 1991, London)

## IN THIS FUGITIVE TIME

Vultures are tearing open a dog's body.
Children still play on hills of garbage
and the green rises anachronistic
in the dead land.

A stench of the world rotting
fills the wind tattered with rags.
A road curves pockmarked.
The violence of the rich covers the poor
in cardboard or bits of tin.
Some one holds up a piece of red plastic
to the setting sun
sinking in the dereliction of the shacks.

My love, have we finally met

in this dust and smoke
in the light of the war piercing
the red sea and the gulf
to take our few steps together
before the siren, the jet
the searchlights on the tarmac
wrench us apart?

In this fugitive time,
our allotted share on earth,
with a world in disarray
that we could not set right,
give me your hand
and let us begin to walk.

(February 1991, Calcutta)

## END NOTES

1.
We met at the edge of the world
in alleys full of debris of the war
the waste of everyday

we came here following
the path of the ball we threw
in a park a long time ago

already

are they calling us?
but our game
had just begun.

2.
The twilight does not hold the names
nor light playing in the leaves
nor the stars in the western sky
know them

the body lies        empty
the house        gutted
charred        butterflies

A madman has sponged
our names
from the slate of memory.


3.
A knife divides the night
bodies from bodies

The world enters into our hearts
like an assassin

What desire in the cool stream
of the dark
with arms severed from the heart
the heart torn
unknown to itself

Warmth rises from bodies
like smoke from the charcoal fire
of the poor

The winter within
freezes our breath.


4.
Who will know our names
in the annals of history

two strangers two lovers
from ends of the earth
meeting in a time of war
started at our birth

Who will listen to the wind
carrying our moans into the night
or see the lightning of our arms
oars in a sea

Who will walk
on the soft carpet of summer nights
which awaits the footsteps
and kisses of lovers
but folds back into itself
the vomit of the drunk and
the desolate bark of little dogs

Who will utter the word
the name that could
have ended the war.

(August 1992, Toronto)

# Mei-mei Berssenbrugge

## THE BLUE TAJ

There is your "dream" and its "approximation."
Sometimes the particular attributes of your labyrinth
seem not so ghastly. More often blue shimmering
walls of the house crack with a sudden drop
in temperature at night, or the builder substitutes
cobalt plaster, which won't hold at this exposure.

Your client vetoes a roof garden, often
because of money, or he likes to kiss you at dawn
and you want to sleep late. Sometimes a person
holds out for the flawless bevelled edge, but might
end up with something half-built, its inlay
scavenged long ago.

Let a ragged edge between the two be lightning
or falling water, and figure its use: the distance
away of a person poised in the air with wings on.
If you string a rope through a pulley at his waist
at least you can lift the New Zealand ferns.
Any fall will *seem* deliberate.

# CHINESE SPACE

First there is the gate from the street, then some flowers inside the wall, then the inner, roofed gate. It is a very plain wall, without expressionistic means, such as contrasting light on paving stones inside the courtyard to the calligraphed foundation stones. My grandfather called this the façade or Baroque experience, rendering a courtyard transparent. The eye expecting to confront static space experiences a lavish range of optical events, such as crickets in Ming jars, their syncopation like the right, then left, then right progress into the house, an experience that cannot be sustained in consciousness, because your movement itself binds passing time, more than entering directs it.

A red door lies on a golden mirror with the fascinating solidity and peacefulness of the pond in the courtyard, a featureless space of infinite depth where neither unwanted spirits nor light could enter directly from outside. It lies within the equally whole space of the yard the way we surrounded our individuals, surrounded by a house we could not wholly retain in memory. Walking from the inner gate across a bridge which crossed four ways over the carp moat, turning right before the ice rink, we pass roses imported from Boston, and enter the main courtyard, an open structure like a ruin. This is not remembering, but thinking its presence around eccentric details such as a blue and white urn turned up to dry, although certain brightnesses contain space, the way white slipcovered chairs with blue seams contain it.

The potential of becoming great of the space is proportional to its distance away from us, a negative perspective, the way the far corner of the pond becomes a corner again as we approach on the diagonal, which had been a vanishing point. The grandmother poses beside rose bushes.

*Mei-mei Berssenbrugge*

That is to say, a weary and perplexing quality of the rough wall behind her gives a power of tolerance beyond the margins of the photograph. Space without expansion, compactness without restriction make this peculiar and intense account of the separable person from her place in time, although many families live in the partitioned house now. The reflecting surface of the pond should theoretically manifest too many beings to claim her particular status in the space, such as a tigerskin in space.

After the house was electrically wired in the thirties, he installed a ticker tape machine connected to the American Stock Exchange. Any existence occupies time, he would say in the Chinese version, reading stock quotations and meaning the simplicity of the courtyard into a lavish biosphere, elevating the fact of its placement to one of our occupation of it, including the macaw speaking Chinese and stones representing infinity in the garden. This is how the world appears when the person becomes sufficient, i.e., like home, an alternation of fatigue and relief in the flexible shade of date trees, making the house part of a channel in space, which had been interior, with mundane fixtures as on elevator doors in a hotel, a standing ashtray that is black and white.
The family poses in front of the hotel, both self-knowing and knowing others at the same time. This is so, because human memory as a part of unfinished nature is provided for the experience of your unfinished existence.

# TAN TIEN

As usual, the first gate was modest. It is dilapidated. She can't tell which bridge crossed the moat, which all cross sand now, disordered with footsteps. It's a precise overlay of circles on squares, but she has trouble locating the main avenue, and retraces her steps in intense heat for the correct entrance, which was intentionally blurred, the way a round arch can give onto a red wall, far enough in back of the arch for sun to light it.

If being by yourself separates from your symmetry, which is the axis of your spine in the concrete sense, but becomes a suspension in your spine like a layer of sand under the paving stones of a courtyard or on a plain, you have to humbly seek out a person who can listen to you, on a street crowded with bicycles at night, with their bells ringing.

And any stick or straight line in your hand can be your spine, like a map she is following in French of Tan Tien. She wants space to fall to each side of her like traction, not weight dispersed within a mirror. At any time, an echo of what she says will multiply against the walls in balanced, dizzying jumps like a gyroscope in the heat, but she is alone.

Later, she would remember herself as a carved figure and its shadow on a blank board, but she is her balancing stick, and the ground to each side of her is its length, disordered once by an armoured car, and once by an urn of flowers at a crossing, because Tan Tien is a park, now. The stick isn't really the temple's bisection around her, like solstice or ancestor. This Tang Dynasty peach tree would be a parallel levitation in the spine of the person recording it.

Slowly the hall looms up. The red stairway's outline gives way to its duration as it extends and rises at a low angle.

In comparison to the family, the individual hardly counts, but they all wait for her at a teahouse inside the wall.

First the gold knob, then blue tiers rise above the highest step, the same colour as the sky.

When one person came to gain its confidence,
she imagines he felt symmetry as flight after his fast among seven meteorites in the dark. He really felt like a globe revolving within a globe.

Even the most singular or indivisible particle or heavenly sphere will adjust when the axis extending beyond itself is pushed, or the sphere it is within is pushed. What she thought was her balance flattens into a stylized dragon on the marble paving stones.

Yet she's reluctant to leave the compound. Only the emperor could walk its centre line. Now, anyone can imagine how it felt to bring heaven news. She is trying to remember this in Hong Kong as the tram pulls suddenly above skyscrapers and the harbour and she flattens against her seat, like a reversal occurring in the poles, or what she meant by, no one can imagine how.

## TEXAS

I used the table as a reference and just did things from there
in register, to play a form of feeling out to the end, which is
an air of truth living objects and persons you use take on,
when you set them together in a certain order, conferring privilege
on the individual, who will tend to dissolve if his visual presence
is maintained, into a sensation of meaning, going off by itself.
First the table is the table. In blue light
or in electric light, it has no pathos. Then light separates
from the human content, a violet-coloured net or immaterial haze, echoing
the violet iceplant on the windowsill, where he is the trace of a desire.

Such emotions are interruptions in landscape and in logic
brought on by a longing for direct experience, as if her memory of experience
were the trace of herself. Especially now, when things have been flying apart in all directions,
she will consider the hotel lobby the incrt state of a form. It is the location
of her appointment. And gray enamel elevator doors are the relational state,
the place behind them being a ground of water or the figure of water. Now,
she turns her camera on them to change her thinking about them into a thought

in Mexico, as the horizon when you are moving can oppose the horizon inside
the elevator via a blue Cadillac into a long traeking shot. You linger
over your hand on the table. The light becomes a gold wing on the table. She sees
it opening, with an environment inside that is plastic and infinite,
but is a style that has got the future wrong.

# *Sadhu Binning*

## A TALE

they made us express the opposing views as well
that's how the matter was initiated
in the gathering

death silenced the laughter
that's how the newcomer was introduced
into the party

midget shadows became tall in seconds
that's how the light was moved around
which fell on them

some houses were illuminated with the outside light
that's how the fire was set
to other people's homes

men became devils instantly after hearing it
that's how the tale of the saint
was related to them

wounds are not drying up but keep on oozing
that's how the ointment on the wounds
has been applied

they are delivering deaths to their own
that's how the light from their eyes
has been stolen

## RIVER RELATIONS

On our way to the randomly chosen spot
where we could see the towering glaciers above
the memory of Gunga Jamna and Sutluj
was not easy to quell

With my brother standing beside me
slowly I dropped the ashes of my father
into the icy water

Now whenever I remember my father
It is the Squamish river I think about
one rupturing relationship
giving birth to a new one

The strangeness of the place melted
a personal image now flows in memory
perhaps that's what my father meant
by relations of rivers to men

## THAT WOMAN

see that woman
the one with large rubber boots
yes! the one crawling in the strawberry row
she is my mother

during lunch breaks
she constantly talks about her village
to escape the pain of burning arthritis

she used to be so self-conscious
back in the old village
she would walk noiselessly
through the village streets

to protect her family's image
of gentleness and nobility

to move forward in the row
she puts pressure on her hurting knees
and each time she lets out a wail

she is my mother


## REBELLIOUS SITA

the man from my village
lives in two eras

after midnight
he comes home drunk
from the local pub
once inside the threshold
he considers himself lord Rama
and demands
his wife be Sita

eyes that have drunk filth all day
see Sita's garment stained
each night the drunkard Rama
wants Sita to walk
through the trial of fire

somewhere
each night
a Sita refuses this scrutiny
and showers questions
on god Rama
and each night
a Rama loses his crown
each morning

religious people gather together
to discuss
how *kalyug* is embezzling
Sita's sense of duty

# Marilyn Chin

## TIENANMEN, THE AFTERMATH

There was blood and guts all over the road.
I said I'm sorry, darling, and rolled over,
expecting the slate to be clean; but she came,
she who was never alive became resurrected.
I saw her in dream . . . a young girl in a *chipao*,
bespeckled, forever lingering, thriving
on the other side of the world, walking in my soles
as I walk, crying in my voice as I cried. When
she arrived, I felt my knuckles in her knock,
her light looming over the city's great hollows.

Hope lies within another country's semaphores.
The Goddess of Liberty, the Statue of Mercy—
we have it all wrong—big boy, how we choose to love,
how we choose to destroy, says Chuangtzu is written
in heaven—but leave the innocent ones alone,
those alive, yet stillborn, undead, yet waiting
in a fitful sleep undeserved of an awakening.

# BEIJING SPRING

Love, if I could give you the eternal summer sun
or China back her early ideological splendour, I would.
If I could hoist the dead horses back
and retrieve the wisdom charred by the pyres of C'hin.
If I could give mother the Hong Kong of her mulberry youth
and father the answers that the ox desired—
—they would still be together now and not blame
their sadness on the unyieldy earth.
If I had separated goose from gander, goose from gander,
the question of monogamy and breeding for life, the question
of the pure yellow seed would not enter.

This courtyard, this fortress,
this alluvium where the dead leave their faces—
each step I take I erase the remnants of another,
each song I sing I obfuscate the song of Changan,
*ripples washing sand ripples washing sand ripples . . .*
each poem I write conjures the dead washing-women of Loyang.

Lover, on Tienamen square, near the Avenue of Eternal Peace,
I believe in the passions of youth,
I believe in eternal spring.
As the white blossoms, sweet harbingers,
pull a wreath around the city,
as heaven spreads its blue indifference over
the bloodied quay, I want to hold you
against the soft silhouettes of my people.
Let me place my mouth over your mouth,
let me breathe life into your life,
let me summon the paired connubial geese
from the far reaches of the galaxy
to soar over the red spokes of the sun's slow chariot
and begin again.

*Marilyn Chin*

# ELEGY FOR CHLOE NGUYEN

(1955-1988)

Chloe's father is a professor of linguistics.
Mine runs a quick-you-do-it Laundromat in Chinatown.
If not pretty, at least I'm clean.

Bipedal in five months, trilingual in a year;
at eleven she had her first lover.

Here's a photo of Chloe's mother in the kitchen
making petit fours, petit fours that are very pretty.
Here's my mother picking pears, picking pears
for a self-made millionaire grower.

The night when Chloe died, her father sighed,
"Chloe was my heart; Chloe was my life!"

One day under an earthen-black sky
and the breeze brushing our adolescent pinafores,
a star fell—or was it a satellite
exploding into a bonfire at the horizon?
Chloe said, "This is how I want to die,
with a bang and not with a flicker."

Oh, Chloe, eternally sophomore and soporific!
Friend of remote moribund languages!
Chloe read Serbo-Croatian, the Latin of Horace.
She understood Egyptian hieroglyphics, the writing of the
tombs.
The tongues of the living, the slangs of the dead—
in learning she had no rival.

Then came the lovers of many languages
to quell her hunger, her despair.
Each night they whispered, "Chloe, you are beautiful."
Then, left her with an empty sky in the morning.
Chloe, can you hear me? Is it better in heaven?

Are you happier in hell? This week I don't understand the  lesson
being a slow learner—except for the one about survival.
And Death, I know him well . . .

He followed my grandfather as a puff of opium,
my father as a brand new car.
Rowed the boat with my grandmother,
blowing gales into my mother's ear.
Wrapped his arms around my asthmatic sister,
but his comforting never won us over.

Yes, Death is a beautiful man,
and the poor don't need dowries to court him.
His grassy hand, his caliph—you thought you could master.

Chloe, we are finally Americans now. Chloe, we are here!

GRUEL

Your name is Diana Toy.
And all you may have for breakfast is rice gruel.
You can't spit it back into the cauldron for it would be unfilial.
You can't ask for yam gruel for there is none.
You can't hide it in the corner for it would surely be found,
and then you would be served cold, stale rice gruel.

This is the philosophy of your tong:
you, the child, must learn to understand the universe
through the port-of-entry, your mouth,
to discern bitter from sweet, pungent from bland.
You were told that the infant Buddha once devoured earth,
and hence, spewed forth the wisdom of the ages.

Meat or gruel, wine or ghee,
even if it's gruel, even if it's nothing,

that gruel, that nothingness will shine
into the oil of your mother's scrap-iron wok,
into the glare of your father's cleaver,
and dance in your porcelain bowl.

Remember, what they deny you won't hurt you.
What they spare you, you must make shine,
so shine, shine . . .

# TURTLE SOUP

*for Ben Huang*

You go home one evening tired from work,
and your mother boils you turtle soup.
Twelve hours hunched over the hearth,
(who knows what else is in that cauldron).

You say, "Ma, you've poached the symbol of long life;
that turtle lived four thousand years, swam
the Wei, up the Yellow, over the Yangtze.
Witnessed the Bronze Age, the High Tang,
grazed on splendid sericulture."
(So, she boils the life out of him).

"All our ancestors have been fools.
Remember Uncle Wu who rode ten thousand miles
to kill a famous Manchu and ended up
with his head on a pole? Eat, child,
its liver will make you strong."

"Sometimes you're the life, sometimes the sacrifice."
Her sobbing is inconsolable.
So, you spread that gentle napkin
over your lap in decorous Pasadena.

Baby, some high priestess has got it wrong.
The golden decal on the green underbelly
says, "made in Hong kong."

Is there nothing left but the shell
and humanity's strange inscriptions,
the songs, the rites, the oracles?

# Madeline Coopsammy

## FIRST HOT DOG

Transporting us to the American Main
it disturbed our island sensibilities
with mindless worship of the American Dream
infusing into our spare and careful island lives
visions of leather-jacketed teens
in tight-hipped jeans
playing chicken on their highways
or hanging out in derelict cars
at local Soda Shoppes.

And the American Dream
was Marlon Brando and Jimmy Dean,
their sultry-eyed surliness
and fleshy mouths
tearing at the heartstrings
of every teenage island girl
black, white, yellow or brown

wishing for the moon.

That day we shared the Dream
in our lean and hungry cafeteria
whose standard fare
of watery juice and sticky "bellyfuls"
never could assuage
the eternal hunger
of growing girls.

And as the uniformed chauffeur

in his Nanny's role
unwrapped the long frankfurters
nestled in their beds of
mustard-smeared wax paper
pungent with onions
and watched
his three red-haired charges
partaking of their movable feast
squabbling and complaining all the while
for a brief moment our glances locked
the black chauffeur and I,
and across the wires
we saw our thoughts
mirrored in each other's eyes

that there were those who ate hot dogs
and those who merely watched.


## NAOMI: WOMAN LOST

Ancestral voices called to her
across Atlantic waters
echoing on her lonely hill
beneath Caribbean skies
and this woman wrapped in jute
her shoulders bare
hair its natural Afro
always smiled benignly
when we came to see her
city children borne like magnet
to the tapia hut
to say, "Morning, Naomi,"
"Morning, children," was all she said.
"She eats her hair," the children whispered,
"though we always leave her food."
And they were proud to show us

this enigma of their hills
and the parents grimly said,
"She was a teacher, once, you know,
until somebody's obeah 'did' for her;
they 'put her so'."
Deep within the forest's silence
its rain-damped earth and tangling creeper
far from the ebb and shout
of island waves
Naomi listened to the river's
muted symphony
and said,
"I'll eat my hair
and wear the robes of my ancestors
and spit upon your world."
But she was wiser than we knew
this woman of the hills
no bag-burdened lady
of the streets she'd be
in dignity and emptiness,
she found another way
until one day
we looked in vain for her
and I, bereft,
wondered why
the ajoupa, too, was gone;
no memory left
no shrine remaining
to Naomi—
lost woman of the hills.

## ROOTS

Rumour had it
that on his deathbed
he sought to make amends
to buy from Heaven
some forgiveness
for the wrong he'd done
and with his worldly wealth
to recompense the daughter
child of the arrowing cane
and indentured servitude
that two-sided coin
of blessing
and of curse,

But her young husband
Dravidian blackness intact
forbade his wife
she of the pink cheeks
and aquiline nose
to reclaim her heritage
jewels, property
and name.

For generations
they forgot the tale
their pride
would not admit the shame
and when others asked
their awkward questions
they refused to answer
preferring to believe
their fabricated truth
to ignore the tell-tale signs

And wanting no part
of English, Irish, Scot
no admission

of ravishment
of tainted blood
they reverted to
the ancestral name.

Now searching for roots
they draw a blank
the unknown Britisher
despoiling a line
went to his Maker
unacknowledged
unforgiven.

## THE SECOND MIGRATION

Was it the bloody-minded Kali
or the many-handed Shiva
who thought it fit to lead us
from the green wastes of the Indo-Gangetic
to the sweet swards of the Caroni
then in a new migration
to Manitoba's alien corn?
They never thought to state
the price to be exacted
or how or where it should be paid.
Images of a just society dangled
tantalizingly before our eyes
we thought that here at last and now at last
the spectres of color
would never haunt
our work, our children's lives, our play
that in the many-faceted mosaic, we—
angled and trimmed to fit—
were sure to find ourselves
our corner of the earth.
How could we not know

that time, which heals
just as frequently destroys
and like the sixties' flower darlings
we, too, must soon become anachronisms
reminders of a time
a time of joy and greening.
We are the mistakes of a liberal time,
you did not really court us, it is true
rather, purging us with neon-colored pills of
medicals and points and two official languages
your tolerant humanity
festered woundings of "brain drain,"
while our leaders pleaded, impotent in agony
"Do not take our best!"
"We want your best,
No Notting Hills for us," you warned.
So once again we crossed an ocean
convinced that little Notting Hills we'd never be.

Now lounging in our bite-sized backyards
and pretending that we do not see
the curling vapours of our neighbor's burger feast
(the third this week)
borne on the Prairie wind across the picket fence—
we ask ourselves how far we are
from San Juan, Belmont and St James.

# Rienzi Crusz

## CONVERSATIONS WITH GOD ABOUT MY PRESENT WHEREABOUTS

True, I have almost forgotten
the terraced symmetries
of the rice-paddy lands.
How the gods underfoot
churned in time
a golden bowl of rice.
A loss of aesthetics, perhaps.

But I am perfect now.
They have crushed the ears of corn
to feed my belly
white slice by slice,
and all imperfections die
with One-A-Day and vitamin B complex.

True, I now walk
without the lumbering skill
of the elephant, the way
he smells the slaughter of mud and hole,
the precision of stars
in this thick legs.

But I am perfect now.
Snow and ice
embrace my horned boots,
skates and skills,
the bones uncracked,
the butterfly's muslin wings

untorn among the thorns.

True, I sometimes ask:
Where's the primal scream
the madness of sun,
the dance of hands and pebbles
by the ocean shore?
And where's the seashell horn,
the words of angels under the sea?

But I am perfect now.
The chameleon
has muted my rowdy scream
to the whisper of a white-boned land,
and stretching in silence,
I am a king of silence.

True, I often miss
the sensuous touch of fingers
on the shying touch-me-not,
the undergrowth's pink badge of bruise,
cacophony of crows,
the rain that pelted my thin bones.

But I am perfect now.
Seduced on shaven grass,
my barbecue glows
like a small hell,
the pork chops kindle,
the Molson cool,
I wear the turban of urban pride.
True, I have changed dead history
to now,
turned my father into me,
the long-gone daddy
now skating on a rink
of clowning children.

But I am perfect now.

I have switched the time and place
of the womb,
my lungs free to scream
though disciplined to whisper,
free to trap the robin in my eye,
if not the strident crow.

I AM perfect now.

A brown laughing face
in the snow,
not the white skull
for the flies
in Ceylon's deadly sun.


## WHERE ADAM FIRST TOUCHED GOD

Junction. The road forks
like a wishbone:
I choose neither, refuse
the destinies in separate highways.
And so I go for the crotch
of no-man's land,
the immediate centre that seems to belong
to no man, and every man.
Here the division ends,
journey's anonymous oasis
where Adam shall continue
his fallen history.

Where the robin shall sing
with the voice of the paddy bird,
the oak wear the fruit of jak,
the crow soar with the eagle;
where the dreaming mind
shall have a choice

of colored snows,
children play with old men,
and the sophisticated young
will again learn their wisdom
from infants, their sanity
from grandfather fables.

I will not travel again
the separate paths of the sun,
the cruel geography of East and West
that blurs the mountain's blue mist
the green of lush valleys below.
Does it matter which way
the road turns,
there will always be another Grail,
another song, another weeping.
Wherever, the wind will never let go
its secrets. Here on undivided ground,
we'll fashion our own mythologies.

## ELEGY

Father,
you were a great mathematician,
loved God and the jambu fruit.

You deserve a poem
exact as the sun,
with no beginning, no end,
just an intense line of light
curving to pure circle.

How can I, a child,
trace even a tangent
to your perfect geometries,
the vast afternoons of your brain

in which you walked so easily
with Euclid and Pythagoras?

And how can I compose
that mathematical prayer
of your living, the way
you chased the ultimate equation,
the something that flowed
from heaven to earth,
earth to heaven?

I'll compose
from the genius of my childhood,
use my crayons to draw the perfect tangent
straight to the tip of your tongue:
Ah, the fruit of jambu!
How I shuddered and shook the tree,
and you and I
shared the sweet red pulp
of our mouths' yearnings.
For the time being, perhaps,
no one will know my real name
or guess where I really come from.
Who'll ever know
that I was once mad
in the carnival of the sun,
when I now live
              without
my loves and hates,
wild lilies or weeds,
only the passion
              of the unsaid word,
the white silence
              of civilization.

# THE RAIN DOESN'T KNOW ME ANY MORE

I, who for so long
shaped the forgotten metaphor:
curved tusks, howdah
and mahout of elephant.
Who splashed the Bird of Paradise
against a cemetery of cars,
sought the root in cabook earth,
the dream     that meandered, got lost
in an orgasm of blood.
I, who held the palm tree's silhouette
against the going sun, a woman,
a child     long enough
to divide a continent,
have new revelations:
I have circled the sun.
The white marshmallow land is now mine,
conquered, cussed upon,
loved.

Look at this other dreaming face,
these new muscles, tempered bones,
black eyes     blue
with a new landscape, legs
dancing the white slopes like a dervish.
Against paddy-bird havocking in tall grass,
bluejay     raucous, cardinals
the color of blood.
For the slow deep rhythms
of the homecoming catamaran,
747 screaming,
wounding the night like a spear.

The monsoon rain
doesn't know me any more:
I am snowbank child, bundled,
with snot under my nose,
white fluff magic in both hands.

Once, rice and curry, passiona juice,
now, hot dogs and fries,
Black Forest Ham on Rye.

So, what's the essential story?
Nothing       but a journey done,
a horizon that would never stand still.


## AFTER THE SNOWFALL

Through garage door lookouts,
winter-hazed:

bleached bones       the catalpa
(without         its green crinoline head)

King maple       so humbled
frail white arms       skying

a tree
praying for its life

Driveway       divided
snow walls       on either side

the Red Sea       parted again
and Moses       nowhere in sight

But Pharaoh       on his snowplough
continues history:       walls the last exit,

laughs: there shall be no diaspora today!

O Lord, mine are summer eyes—
tomorrow       the promised land?

your Egypt       still shimmers and shines
in its white       misery

# Cyril Dabydeen

## FOR COLUMBUS

### I.

When grapes are her breasts
And apples her skin, I am at home—
I long for Italian brothers, Greek sisters,
An African father
                    an Indian mother.

I long with the same longing
As the clouds looking down, the sky
About to tilt over
Like a ship in a hefty sea.

I also long for a French aunt
Who will elegantly raise a handkerchief
In the wind, signalling an archipelago—
And I cry out, "Islands, islands!"

### II.

Now it is you who I remember,
Your neck bruised, the shadow
Of an axe coming down
                    in the Tower.

You too, Cortez, as Montezuma burns
Inside, his cry resounding in the night,
You with your Quetzalcoatl face,
A helmet still glinting.

Pizarro next,
As I watch the Incas in silver mines
Living out a life, buried in sand, their heads
Above the ground while the ocean once more
                threatens disaster.


III.


With a Crusoe mask, I listen in the distance,
Our Friday's commands,
The Spanish Empire sinking in the background—
This treasure is all I am left with,
Bible in hand, the sun whipping by—
A lopsided moon sinking lower
Into a bottomless sea,

And I try to jump over it, my paradiso,
EL Dorado, the heathen sky
Falls prostrate
                at my feet.


# DECLARATION

This declaration of possibilities,
it is the way with metaphors,
weighing reforestation like antlers.

Such verbs,
this bush camp's sweat,
hewing out of solid wood

Or being up at five in the morning
and preparing to take
the woodpecker by surprise.

All sound without fury—
I am hardly at rest
at Trapper Lake

Believe it or not
as I am pigeonholed
a prairie poet by Revenue Canada.

I am prouder yet of my heritage
and those who came and listened,
the Lakehead scholars—

Who have eased the anger
out of me since the beginning—
now find me mellow

Like Suknaski's disdain
with harmonica strumming—
he being less Ukrainian.

I succumb for a while—
this style is all
I am left with

Eager as I am to read on,
my dialect's best
even as I pretend.

# MY MOTHER

## I.

I am doing it again:
I've fallen into the old trap,
telling my mother
she must forsake the old ways,
she must go out in the snow
day or night and start jogging.

She who has lived most of her life in the tropics,
raising her children, us,
having toiled all the years long;
suddenly I want her to be in the fashion magazines,
to live her life with panache, be confident,
or overbearing in her dealings with other people;

Never to be a quiet woman any more,
as I tell her to change her diet in Canada
so as to overcome stress—
to exercise regularly. She must!
She balks, though never protesting loudly,
and she yearns to do as I tell her—
I, her eldest, who has attended university,
who figures he knows it all—
what's best for her because I have been here longest;

Telling her again and again, as brothers and sisters
listen, and say I'm too demanding—
yet I continue to berate her each time I visit,
imagining a life of newness, her changed behaviour.
See, we're in Canada, the Great White North!
This is the land of people taking control,
land of people living with determined zest,
people always in command, controlling destiny—
. . . but she quickly laughs
and tells me to mind my manners, finally.

II.

That night I imagine my mother skiing,
coming down a mountain with breakneck speed
as she loudly calls out to me,
then telling the others what she's achieved;
but I see her tumble and fall,
but she is miraculously up again—

Making her mark on the prismatic Canadian
landscape or soil, where else?
Who can doubt her zest?
Who can blame her for not trying hard?

A gin and tonic next.
I mull over my words, feeling guilty,
thinking I must leave her alone
in her silence, her memory intact,
despite her daily watching soap opera,
and all other acts on the TV—
still in deepest silence
in the regular living room.

My siblings, they mutter softly,
sometimes alone with her when I'm not there
as she yet ponders going out when the wind whistles—
the cold and the snow piling up—
imagining the outside with closed eyes,
her brows furrowed,
eyes dilating next, blinking,
as in the everlasting tropical sun.

# HORSES IN THE DARK

*For Timothy Findley*

This instinct compelling us to believe—
mementoes of shapes as we dwell on
more than memory; hoofbeats all around,
the ground overwhelming us at a glance.

The light's dazzling speed with bat or owl;
other creatures that we call our own
and are not as we inhale the stale air,
the sea at our command like a further miracle.

We genuflect with the sun coming down,
the trees spreadeagling shadows . . .
the leaves' own choir in variegated music,
as the horses lunge forward with trajectory

Or circular movement; arabesques, shadows without
the sense of oblivion because of hopes we cherish,
being finally here as the ground seeps in;
now the anxieties of our age with offsprings

Watching us as we try to redeem ourselves,
contemplating aspirations with other rhythms
keeping us honed in: emotions paralyzing us
because of who we are. The horses go round and round,

Heads raised, fire coming from their nostrils—
they attempt to leap off the ground, Pegasus-like;
instincts we now know are too precious
for us to make much use of, the light startling us

With a speed we never thought previously possible.

# MY SUNDRY LIFE

My sundry life
I've given over
to wielding in a storm
with pellets of rain
    —and everywhere
the meandering self in green.

I murmur regret
    in an alligator creek
with star-shaped ripples;
    I bend and circle—
a dogfish flotilla
    in my midst
scattering fragments of the sun,

Glinting more of my life
    with thunder-belch
and forest spell.
    I listen with continuing awe
pressing an ear to the ground,
    my heart beating further rain.

Such is my beloved,
    my eyes plastered
with clay—
a memory song once again
    my sounds of soil & floating things
in the everlasting presence
    of dreams gone haywire
on this one-time
    homing ground.

# Chitra Banerjee Divakaruni

## MAKING SAMOSAS

We sift salt into chapati flour, pour oil
and skin-warm water. *Punch it*
*more, more,* my mother says. *The trick*
*is to get all the kinks out*
*before you start.* The filling
is already cooling, spread on
the round tin tray on the counter
where this winter day the late sun
catches it briefly, the warm yellow
potatoes, the green glint of peas. She
rolls out the dough that I have made
into little balls, her circles perfect

as in my childhood. *The doctor said*
*he wasn't to have any,* she says.
*But what rages he would fly into*
*if we tried to stop him. Remember*
*that time on your birthday*
*when he threw the chutney bowl*
*clear across the room?*
My father, whom we have not seen
these seven years
who hung up each time we called

even after his stroke. I stir
tamarind into the chutney and see him
as she does,
in his kitchen 1500 miles away
his left leg dragging a little.

He peers into the leached white light
of a refrigerator, reaches for
a carton, a bottle. Around him
a city of silent, falling snow.
*Stuff carefully,* she says, *press too hard
and they'll fall apart.* The oil ready

she slides the samosas in, one by one.
They puff up crisp and golden
hissing. I lift them
with a slotted spoon and drain them
on newspapers. Her back to me
my mother washes her hands
letting the water run and run. The kitchen
fills with the old brown smell
of roasted cumin, crushed cilantro leaves.

## INDIGO*

Bengal, 1779-1859

The fields flame with it, endless, blue
as cobra poison. It has entered
our blood and pulses
up our veins like night. There is
no other color. The planter's whip
splits open the flesh of our faces,
a blue liquid light trickles
through the fingers. Blue dyes the lungs
when we breathe. Only the obstinate eyes

refuse to forget where once the rice
parted the earth's moist skin
and pushed up reed by reed,

green, then rippled gold
like the Arhiyal's waves. Stitched
into our eyelids, the broken dark,
the torches of the planter's men,
fire walling like a tidal wave that
flattened the ripe grain with a smell
like charred flesh, broke
on our huts. And the wind
screaming in the voices of women
dragged to the plantation,
feet, hair, torn breasts.

In the worksheds, we dip our hands,
their violent forever blue,
in the dye, pack it
in great embossed chests
for the East India Company.
Our ankles gleam thin blue
from the chains. After that night
many of the women killed
themselves. Drowning
was the easiest.
Sometimes the Arhiyal gave us back
the naked, bloated bodies, the faces
eaten by fish. We hold on
to red, the color
of their saris, the marriage mark
on their foreheads,
we hold it carefully inside
our blue skulls, like a man
in the cold *Paush* night
holds in his cupped palms
a spark, its welcome scorch,
feeds it his foggy breath
till he can set it down
in the right place,
to blaze up and burst
like the hot heart of a star
over the whole horizon,

a burning so beautiful you want it
to never end.
* Indigo planting was forced on the farmers of Bengal, India, by
the British, who exported it as a cash crop for almost a hundred
years until the peasant uprising of 1860, when the plantations were
destroyed.


# THE BRIDES COME TO YUBA CITY

The sky is hot and yellow, filled
with blue screaming birds. The train
heaved us from its belly
and vanished in shrill smoke.
Now only the tracks
gleam dull in the heavy air,
a ladder to eternity, each receding rung
cleaved from our husbands' ribs.
Mica-flecked, the platform
dazzles, burns up through thin
*chappal* soles, lurches
like the ship's dark hold,
blurred month of nights, smell of vomit,
a porthole like the bleached iris
of a giant unseeing eye.

Red-veiled, we lean into each other,
press damp palms, try
broken smiles. The man
who met us as the ship whistles
a restless *Angrezi* tune
and scans the fields. Behind us,
the black wedding trunks, sharp-edged,
shiny, stenciled with strange men-names
our bodies do not fit into:
*Mrs Baldev Fohl, Mrs Kanwal Bains.*

Inside, folded like wings,
bright salwar kameezes scented
with sandalwood. For the men,
kurtas and thin white gauze
to wrap their uncut hair.
Laddus from Jullundhar, sugar-crusted,
six kinds of lentils, a small bag
of bajra flour. Labelled in our mothers'
hesitant hands, pickled mango and lime,
packets of seeds—methi, karela, saag—
to burst from this new soil
like green stars.

He gives a shout, waves
at the men, their slow
uneven approach. We crease our eyes
through the veils' red film,
cannot breathe. Thirty years
since we saw them. Or never,
like Harvinder, married last year
at Hoshiarpur to her husband's photo,
which she clutches tight to her
to stop the shaking. He is fifty-two,
she sixteen. Tonight—like us all—
she will open her legs to him.

The platform is endless-wide.
The men walk and walk
without advancing. Their lined,
wavering mouths, their
eyes like drowning lights.
We cannot recognize a single face.

NOTE: Yuba City in northern California was settled largely by Indian railroad workers around the 1900s. Due to immigration restrictions, many of them were unable to bring their families over—or, in the case of single men, go back to get married—until the 1940s.

# I, MANJU

(after Mira Nair's film *Salaam Bombay!*)

1.
The bed smells of crushed jasmine,
my mother's hair,
the bodies of strange men.
All day she lies
against the pillow's red velvet.
Smoke rings fly up, perfect ovals
from her shining mouth. Sometimes
she tells me shadow stories,
butterfly fingers
held against the light.
On the panes, silver snakes
of rain. The curtains
flap their wild wet wings.
My friend the tea boy
brings us sweet steaming chai
from the shop below.
She lets me drink from her glass,
wipes the wet from his hair.
Turns up the radio. A song
spills into us.
She claps in time and laughs.
We dance and dance
around the bed
as though the rainbow music
will never end.


2.
From the balcony, my waiting
probes the swollen night.
Like light down a tunnel
she disappears.into the room,
each time with a different
man. My fingers

squeeze the rails
till rust scars the palms.
The door shuts. The curtains
shiver with the silhouettes.
My nails are cat-claws
on the panes. Tinkle of glass,
a sharp curse, thick men-sounds
like falling.
After a long time
my feet find the way
to the street-children.
They let me lie with them
on newspaper beds,
do not ask. My face tight
against the tea boy's
cool brown spine. My arms.
I, Manju. All the dark
burns with the small animal sounds
from my mother's throat.

## THE MAKERS OF CHILI PASTE

The old fort on the hill
is now a chili factory
and in it, we
the women,
saris tied over nose and mouth
to keep out the burning.

On the bare brown ground
the chilies are fierce hills
pushing into
the sky's blue. Their scarlet
sears our sleep.
We pound them into powder
red-acrid as the mark
on our foreheads.

All day the great wood pestles
rise and fall,
rise and fall,
our heartbeat. Red
spurts into air, flecks our arms
like grains of dry blood.
The color will never
leave our skins.

We are not like the others
in the village below,
glancing bright black
at men
when they go to the well for water.

Our red hands
burn like lanterns
through our solitary nights.
We will never
lie breathless
under the weight of thrusting men,

birth bloody children.

We are the makers of chili paste.
Through our fingers
the mustard oil seeps
a heavy, melted gold. In it
chili flecks swirl and drown.
We mix in secret spices,
magic herbs,
seal it in glowing jars
to send throughout the land.
All who taste our chilies
must dream of us,
women with eyes like rubies,
hair like meteor showers.
In their sleep forever
our breath will blaze
like hills of chilies
against a falling sun.

# Ramabai Espinet

## HOSAY NIGHT

Like a key turning
In the rusty iron lock of memory
Shadows filter past the thin
Skinless eye of moon now
Cutting through the knife-blue sky
And, like echoes off an old skin drum
Drawn across the lash of memory
The mind pitter-patters . . .

Hosay night in deep-edged
St James dark where
Drumsticks rain fire on Potoy's back
I was a small boy on Flag Night
A small girl on Ganges Street
Watching the tadjahs, near the mosque door
The sun and moon kissed
Straw fires lined the streets

Stirring a dim morning dream
Of colder times, ancient streets,
Fires for warming hands, and drums,
Tribesmen, plainsmen, my grandfather's
Pale eyes and swarthy hands . . .
A journey outside the lodge
Of memory, the cutting edge
Of bitter cane

Behind the moon and God's back
Pain knowing no end

We lived alone, like
Shadow murdering shadow
The stars alone for safety
Tassas beating in the dark
Rum, stickfight, chulhahs
Flights to nowhere

This land is home to me
Now homeless, a true refugee
Of the soul's last corner
Saddhu days and babu days
And Mai in ohrni days
Lost to me—like elephants
And silks, the dhows of Naipaul's
Yearning, not mine

# IN THE MONTH OF THE STURGEON MOON

Love, stranger than any fictions
Of imagination or certitude
Invaded me in this month of reckoning
When I, stalled on a plateau
Whose scarred rockjaw held
More alien secrets than my
Own rock-stones could ever tell,
Stabbed the air and barked
Furiously after unheld truths

This the month of a shift
In the sands of timely deserts
In the blue of ocean waves
And the inescapable silt of deltas
The boots in the desert lie
Soles upward—their bent toes
Tell the story of upturned grief

And if one morning I sit under a
Treeless tent—far from any
River, distances like moon
From rock lobster and sand crab
And unfurl my bitter wand
If on that morning my tears
Brine and sour sea grapes
Turn to sulphurous acid
And eat the anger
Out of steel-blue eyes

If such acid cleave
In two his forked tongue
My spume and spittle would begin
Again—after such little waste—
To break into its wattled life
On the margins

A levelling of the lonely toil
Of placid earth
Curling the edges of history
Lighting a flambeau high
Over storm and dew
Singing Om, Shanti, Om

And what constellations
Still unformed
Along the arcing slant
Of the known world, lingering
At the sudden corners
Of moonrise in Muskoka
Niagara, Gananoque, Kahnasakawe
Old gods and tilting futures
And phantom shadows warning
Of some things more macabre
By far
Than those held in dreams

I dream of waves like

Tidal fancies lashing
The bed of ocean and
Casting, at last, only
Sour sea grapes
Bitter almonds, rubbed
Donkey eyes to the light
On the vagrant sand

When rocks signal their
Foresight and the dawn curfew
Breaks: new soldiers and sentries
—Ours through time—
Invade our sights
Our land, our own
All monuments, all history
All earth.

# MARRONNAGE

*For Elvira*

That day I walked, alone
Dust in my nostrils
My throat parched sand
My thoughts
Empty of everything
Except a lust
To walk forever
On the long road
To Manzanilla

Walking through
That winding coconut road
To a place where
You turned a shadowy corner
And disappeared . . .

Death, trailing his robes,
Your blood-soaked shroud
Trailing
In the dust

We walked
In single file
You out of sight
Just beyond the Traveller's Palm . . .
Basil, indolent, flowing
In high style,
Me, struggling
Big belly tied
To rest the child

Hurry, hurry
Around the black sage bush
Down by the stretch of water
You, just ahead . . .
My shoes lost
Hair loosening
Hurry, hurry
In the Cocal
You must be waiting

# LIZ

She stands
A wraith
Waiting for a sexual benediction
A pale ghost wrapped
Around a fig plant in moonlight

Somewhere
On the low hills of St. Thomas
Hearing a longing
In the wind, smelling
A bouquet of wild herbs

A fragrance in the air
Redolent of spices
Amaranth and frangipani
Jump-up-and-kiss-me
Wild pumpkins and plums

Longing for rest
For a place
In a Caribbean sea
Of changes
And quadrilateral curves

Blowing her way:
A Gothic wind
Full of longing
For sinfulness
Beyond orgasm

Her senses
Stretching for miles
A man—primal, sweet
No other gifts
Primal, sweet

In the coal-tar bucket

Of his lingering days
He will perceive
This wraith
A Gothic plaint

From an old dream
Wrapped over
And around him
Herself erased
Beyond history

In her dream of sinfulness—
Easing
Out of complacency
Arms black
And tangled

Liana vines
A body lashing
Like rain
On the low hills
Of St. Thomas

Out of a seepage
Of legend
Gothic, strange
She affixes her
Longing

She stares—a wraith—
Her hair wrapped
Around tomorrow
Waiting for blessing
In a dream of sinfulness

# Lakshmi Gill

## THE MAN WITH A MISSION

From the pulpit at Sunday Mass,
the special priest visiting from the missions,
drumming up business, says: "And Mary
must've been *physically* beautiful
because she was the Mother of God."
From my lowly pew, I look up in shock,
I, deflated and askew, from surgery, ugly with sin.

He continues: "And her skin was fair and firm,"
and I, dark and wrinkled with punishment
(six months, the surgeon said, before you'll see
a form shape up again). "And she was born
all beautiful all at once, once and for all time,"
like a concept in God's mind, unblemished,
no metastasizing cancer to alter her ineluctably.

"*Physically*," he insists, as if we had already forgotten
the *blut und boden* image, and shivers run around
the numb thigh where morphine hit when I see
this special man among the vile brown faces
festered with sores he must clean to restore
to that immaculate state of Beauty.

# TIME EXPIRED

Coins click. The metal finger
swings to the end. It begins
to die as soon as it is born.
Nascentes morimur, said Manilius.
Backwards, back to the beginnings
A rigid mobile moving in the half light
above the lonely crib. A tube in the wet womb.
A nothing before its creation.

I run around in the shops of life
pitched forward against the beat
edging towards death. I run to cheat it
of one second in a dying hour.
Armed with my worldly goods, my comforts,
I make this gasp at death's door,
this costly victory. I scoff, I grin
at time before its expiration.

# JUST THIS

It's just the night, isn't it?
You know the night. This is dark.
It comes after light.
You've seen the light, haven't yon?
You remember the forsythia in the sun.
How you looked up from your waiting
astonished by the wild yellow buds
at a time when you thought nothing
could ever astonish you again.

It's just the rain, isn't it?
You can't have forgotten that.
Not here, in Vancouver, where it rains and rains.
No, you can't see it now but it's there—

thin, just moist at the hair of your skin.
If you should step out and touch a leaf,
you'll feel just a slight shiver like fright.

It's just the silence, isn't it?
You know this quiet. It comes before
the morning birds that call you out of fitful sleep.
You hear your breath.
It's just your breath in the silence.
You hold it in stasis and wonder how it stays there
motionless and still as if it were dead.

It's just the end of the day, isn't it?
You earned your keep, you fed the children,
you cracked a joke, you brushed your teeth.
At six in the evening, you had black tea.
You drank tea and wondered what happened
to the first sentences, the poems in the shower,
the words meant to be written down after work
except there was no after work until you thought,
ah well—in time—what did it matter?

It's just the time, isn't it?
You know time well.
It's always Tuesday, the day your sister died,
and all this time just echoes of that one day.
It's just the dying echo hushing away. The one long sigh.
This is the night, the rain, the silence, the end, the time.
That's all.

# I TURN

As if I could have stopped it from changing
when all about it was changing furiously
at all times of the day, a relentless
beat beating all about it. As if it would
have turned around at my commanding voice
and reared up while the other chargers charged
hither, thither in massacred confusion.
The way led to that other direction, I said.
I said, look that's the gate to the city.
It looked and went on with its metamorphosis.

I don't know when it got away from me
or if I even had a say in it, say,
a little say in its transformations.
Or maybe, I had a lot to do with it,
the lot of persons inside knocking about
bumping themselves into conclusions. But,
the point is, it seems to go on and on
with its paisley figures, pale copies of what
I consider The Real Me, deeply hidden
in the structured sonnet's elegant rhyme.

Ha ha. I blush to reveal my contours
when the mountain has levelled into wide
valleys and slipped up to the other side
and down again, dingdong avalanches.
As if I could have foreseen the tribulations,
fibrillations, downright revolutions,
the cups of tea, the tea leaves in the compost,
at night while I turned in bed waiting for dawn
thinking who are these shades, who is this woman?

# Kimiko Hahn

## THE CRAB

Good thing my daughter is clever
as my husband is stupid. In the market last week
she took pity on a crab about to be speared,
bought it and let it go by the bay.
Some way to spend your money,
but it's your business, I told her.
That same day as my husband was hoeing
he saw a snake about to devour a frog.
He tried to stop it by pulling the frog back
with the tip of the hoe
but it was already half inside the snake's mouth.
Out of compassion he cried: Snake,
let it go and I'll give you my daughter.
To his surprise, the snake disgorged the green thing
and slithered off.
That night a gentleman came for our daughter.
My husband managed to gain a night
before he took her forever.
Meanwhile my daughter discovered his idiotic pledge
and hid in our chest.
The next night the snake returned as a snake
slunk under the door and banged on the chest
with its hefty tail.
Help me please! our daughter cried
but it seemed her fate was sealed.
Just then a small image of Kannon appeared
telling her not to worry.
Soon, a hundred crabs
crawling through every window and crack

tore the snake into shreds and left.
I turned back to my cooking.


## THE FAN

Walking along Suzaku Avenue I met a woman
as ravishing as the twilight
over dark winter branches,
as those orange clouds, as the breeze
lifting dust by my geta.
I needed her and told her she equalled the Sun Goddess
in complexion and character.
She smiled faintly in the dusk,
her red lips juicy as I imagined her sex
and soon we were off hand-in-hand
down a back street to her room.
As I began to unwrap the silks off her breasts and hips
taste the buds of her nipples,
she told me we couldn't make love ever
or I would die. *Crazy woman, prick tease,* I thought
and the fire under my skin burned off my clothes
till I was at the point of entry.
All right, she said with a coolness
that burned like ice on the tongue.
*Take me but know that I shall die in your place.*
What melodrama! I smiled and, her skin as soft as fur pelts,
I sank into her for what seemed hours.
After, we lay back dripping with sweat
to talk as true lovers will, of our most secret desires.
Well, I guess I spoke most of my need for her only her
like the singers often sing.
She smiled again and asked for my fan.
*Surely you have not forgotten I shall die in your place.*
*Find me in Butoku Hall.* She vanished
without even opening the door. Not a trace of her in the alley.
I ran to Butoku Hall. There on the floor
lay a bloody fox with a fan over its face.

Forever grateful every night I copy the Lotus Sutra
dedicating it to her memory, that in the figure I knew
she will rise to the heavens with wings like fans.


## A CIRCLE OF LANTERNS

Walking through a light rain
that quenches even the pavement
we turn from the funeral service
toward a Chinese banquet where
we will eat tofu, rice and vegetables
prepared in seven different ways.
En route my older child asks
why grandma's body was not at the temple
and I am cornered by her need for reasons:

"Because grandma wished to be cremated.
After death the body can't feel anything—"
"Like hair?"
"Yes, like hair. So the body
is placed in a special fire
that releases the spirit, leaving only ashes.
Grandma's ashes are in a box at the temple."
She is silent, then:
"Some people say dead people are reborn."
"Some people believe that. I believe
grandma is now wind, sunlight and moonlight."
She adds after dinner, "And mist."

The reverend explains that the Bon Festival this July
will be our mother's hatsu bon: the first time
we dress in kimono, pin up our hair and rouge our cheeks
to dance under the circle of lanterns for her
as she taught me in Kahului when I was four.
When I was ready to learn everything.

# THE UNBEARABLE HEART

In the train an hour along the Sound, distant from the details of grief
I look up from the news toward the salt marshes
clumped beneath a snow we thought we would not see this year;
snow fallen twice this past week since mother died, instantly, 10:35 pm,
broadsided by an Arab kid fleeing a car of white kids with baseball
                                                 bats;

a snow only matched by my father's head as I reach to touch him
as I have never touched him. He wishes
he could see her once more, to say goodbye,
as Ted and I said goodbye to the body that was mother's.
Grief comes in spasms: the smell of banana bread, I think of the
                                          rotting fruit
my sister and I tossed before father came home from Yonkers General.
A flashlight. The flashlight she bought my youngest daughter
who always rummaged for one under grandpa's side of the mattress.
The orange day lilies the florist sent to our apartment:
the lilies from the woods she brought to my wedding.

And after I told my six-year-old, grandma died in the accident,
after tears and questions she suggested, maybe now
                        is a good time
to explain what the man has to do with babies.
So I chose one perfect lily from that vase
and with the tip of a paring knife slit open the pistil
to trace the passage pollen makes to the egg cell—
the eggs I then slipped out and dotted on her fingertip, their
greenish white translucent as the air in this blizzard that cannot
                               cool the unbearable heart.

*As I write this, I still demand your attention, mother.*

And now that she's gone how do we find her—
especially my small daughters who will eventually recall their
                                 grandmother
not as a snapshot in the faults of the mind
but as the incense in their hair long after the reading of the Lotus Sutra

Kimiko Hahn

# INSTEAD OF SPEECH

The reflection of Noh actors
in the reflecting pool, the torches,
the faces all turned in one direction
make your heart throb:
*this is home.* This is home the way a home
will never admit you
because you are by definition alien and female.

No matter what (bitchy, manipulative, fertile,
on top)
you girl
are the vulnerable one by social
and biological inheritance.
At the moment.

*All women are streetwise,* she said
And, *the penis is the linchpin*
*of linguistic systems.* Funny

the word penis.

He recognized the comb as something
you bought for the honeymoon you didn't take.
After the separation
his girlfriend interfered with your grief
so you wanted—to what?

The actor's feet never left the ground
as he slowly whirled across the wooden stage
towards anything.

All summer you wore your husband's gym shorts and
t-shirts
*You wear that outside?* your sister asked.
A man on the stoop called: *too much meat for the street.*

Carpenters construct a stage

so stamping and pounding resound
like the chest cavity.
I'm told ceramic urns are planted beneath
in strategic locations.

    On a subway poster of a voluptuous woman
    someone drew in tits
    and a cock stuck up her ass. *Had it been a man*
    there might be a cock stuck in his mouth
    not a cunt.
    The evermore unattached phallus.

    —so you wanted to rip her fucking face off—

A woman with short blonde hair and white earrings
entered the cafe.
She wore an immaculate white t-shirt
and you knew were you a lesbian and she were
you would approach her
and court her.

There are only actors
yet so many female roles
so many women's masks it hurts.
I would like to climb the stage
in white tabi and silk
stretch my arms out—fingers together palms down—
and stamp.
Calling out: *nantoka nantoka saro*

    like sorrow, sorrow sorrow

# Garrett Hongo

## MINISTRY: HOMAGE TO KILAUEA

*Thinking about volcanoes gives me hope—*
                                    *all the pure of it*

When my two boys were babies, to help them fall asleep in the
        afternoons,
I liked driving them out from the house we always rented in
                Mauna Loa Estates,
up the highway a mile or so through the park entrance,
then plunging down past all the micro-climates and botanical
                                                realities
until I got to the swing in the road just before the turnout to
                Kilauea observatory at Uwekahuna,
where I could pull over into a little gravel slot by the roadside
        and let all the airconditioned tour buses
                and shining red rental cars
                and USGS Cherokees and geologists' Broncos swoosh by
while I took a long view
over the saddle towards the veldt-like lower slopes of Mauna Loa
        my boys already asleep in the back seat.

        What I liked was the swoop of land,
the way it rolled out from under my beach-sandalled feet,
        and the swimming air,
                        freighted with clouds
                that seemed the land's vision rising over it.

I could have been the land's own dream then,
and I liked thinking of myself that way,
as offspring come to pay it the tribute of my own thoughts,

little brainy cyclones
that touched down in the lava channels
                          or drained back into rivulets of wind.
"Cloud and Man differ not," I joked to myself,
"All is One under Heaven." And why not?

What if we were to recast ourselves as descendants
all gathered at the foot of our heresiarch mountains,
drawn by a love like primitive magnetisms and convection currents
          calling all things back to their incarnate sources? Our
lives might be ordered by a conscious abstinence,
a year of giving up to save for a trip home.
We would sacrifice for an earthbound commitment—

                          homage to birthplace,
source rock come up from a star's living depth.

What would be the point other than to step into the sulfuric
                          cleansing of volcanic clouds?
Our dithyrambs of dream-mountains not quite earth's equal
but more vague than that—like clouds around Mauna Loa,
drifting continents of vapour and dust
riding the gyring wind gusts over Halemaumau and Iki,
mantling of evanescence on the tropical shoulders of an angel?

Aren't we the earth become known to itself,
we celebrants of a sublime not completely dreadful,
but companionable too, its presence like two sleeping children,
innocent dragons
                          fogging the car's rear window with a visible breath?

# Kevin Irie

## CHRONOLOGY

Come spring, and the waters
blackened with life—
midges and catfish clouded warm pools.
Tadpoles hung like dark tears
in the pond where
duckweed, waterborne
twin of clover, floated in rafts,
a jigsaw assembled by
wind and current, dangling pale roots,
legs of a mayfly.

Come summer, and the shallows
filled up with nymphs
armoured in chitin, each body
a lance, jousting
beneath the face of the water
while pads of lilies
floated above them
like dark full moons adrift on the pond.

Then came drought:
mudbanks riddled with tunnels for flies,
worms exposed as small white roots. ·
Sunfish baked on the mud,
rotted, their stench held fast
on ivory prongs.

After, came autumn,
clouded with rain,

the monotone chant of the
cold north wind driving the song
of the finches south.
Leaves chose
to drown in cider-dark water,
to sink their brilliance into the mud.
Dusk, on its long journey back to the north,
nested in shadows, routed
out warmth.

Now, comes winter, an ice
that fractures the pond in silence,
renders a stratum
of dense white quartz.
Reeds turn to straw, a blind for the wind
that hunts for the frog
asleep under ice,
its pickle skin buried
deep in the mud,
its bloodstream: a current
that courses toward spring.

## AN IMMIGRANT'S SON VISITS THE HOMELAND

You are the future
these fathers dream of: the son
who flies over for a summer visit,
his belly nourished by Canadian wheat,
the one who is welcomed
into the garden, given the shade,
the head of the table.

You are the stranger
whose past is dark
as the hairs that sprout
beneath your fine shirt;

the boy who speaks English
just as well as the Yankees
that inhabit their TV screens at night.

Daughters increase
the light in their eyes
as if your words
were fuel for desire:
that one word, *Canada,*
crumbling in their mouths
like sweetened morsels of heady cake.

They know the locals
who offer them marriage
can only give love
and food, at best.

But English, they know,
is better than food:
it's the field that grows
a good many crops over and over,
the seed that can raise
a stalk unto heaven.

And these girls are restless,
tired of a future
handed down to their mothers:
the soil that is drained from too much planting,
the days that drop
like fruit to the ground,
sometimes eaten, sometimes gnawed.

They want your life
to be their future,
press ripe slices
of fruit to your hands.

*Look,* their eyes seem to say to you,
*English is our aphrodisiac.*

# FLIGHT: AN IMMIGRANT'S MEMORY

How much descends
with a sight, a sound?

The pigeons that flew
in and out of your childhood

now settle on telephone wires
above you.

The clucking of hens
in Kensington Market

captures your past
in one light cage

small enough
to be carried by hand.

You've made the long
migration through words

to finally arrive, at home
with English,

a species of language
that flocks the world over,

a dominant breed.

But looking at streets .
in downtown Toronto,

where feathers of frost
are pressed to March windows,

and soot discolors
the last April snow,

part of you lifts
at the thought of the Old World,

then circles

      and circles

with no place to land.

## THE CAMPS: BURNING THE DEAD

Because there was no undertaker,
no place
allotted to the dead
as yet,

inmates had to cremate
each body
as quickly as possible,
recruiting
boys
to watch the pyre
which often took all night to burn.

It was their job
to guard the corpse,
stoke the flames
when the fire bled low,

each one serving
an hour's endurance
then relieved, and coming
back

with ashes
sewn so deep in their clothes

that finally their own garments
were burned as well.

Now, years later,
it is another memory
that men retain
but seldom tell,

tailored
in their suits
at another funeral,

their past

still sewn deep in their skin.

## HEARTS

The pond holds that past
we do not remember,
that self which abandoned
its fins and gills,

stranding the heart
alone in darkness
to struggle on in its own
salt pool.

There is no light
in the heart, or water.
The sun can be dimmed
on the pond each night,
only a ghost of its own true self.
And what of the heart—
that puff of red smoke

in the side of a sunfish
struggling upwards,
tugged to the light—

what do we make of
its cloudy red ink,
the small crumpled ball
of scarlet chiffon in the
side of a belly,
filling with air?

Or cut to our own heart,
locked under flesh,
moist as a fish and
gulping at blood,

still loyal to what
unknown tides we've forgotten,
afloat in the small dark pond
it calls home,

keeping the beat
that measures out life,
the countdown to infinity.

# Sally Ito

CHANSON

> when we sing
the small beauty and rage
of the heart

> > the hand trembles to touch
the clock that is ticking there

Time
the beat of it in words
is the only human act
> that arrests it   briefly

But a respite   as powerful

as the first storm
> that created the world
that brought forth
the trilling bird
> the singing wave

that shaped from dust
this hollow mouth
into sound

# HAECCEITAS

Suchness,
the way of things
*in* things

Driving by stubbled fields under pale blue sky
in the cold clear afternoon in November,
there are dogs    farm dogs
half mangy, black white brown yellow mutts
        ambling in ditches
                sniffing the sky
                        chasing speedy nothings
                                rolling in the dry grass.

They are in their state.                    *Haecceitas*

Undisturbed in their element
bliss in their blood
undetected but for
        this eye
that passes like sudden flame
to fire their beings
into this quiet art
which is the poet's own private
*haecceitas.*

# SEAHORSE

Its delicacy
        is the poet's,
the selfish concerns    indulgences
curved into a tight tail
that winds
around the most fragile
tendril of seaweed.

The eyes are dumb, mute
and the snout a long hollow tube
from which the music
of bubbles appear    disappear.

This breath is just enough

to bring forth the froth
of some sweltering sea thought

    and set into motion
the slim, quivering wisp of its
    briny messenger.


## THE POOR

all that they asked was that we should continue to remember the
poor . . .               *Galatians 2:10*


Without their nourishment,
where would we be?

Bloated without sense,
raw pouches of watery wealth
wind-pockets of words
sandbags of sleeping inertia
shored up, shored up, shored up

against some tide that will never come.

*The poor are always with us*

as if they had never been,
as if our eyes had only been fixed on the sky

Where are they who are our mirrors
sleeping in the small shade of our luxuries,
the salt in our satin?

When we look at them without flinching
into the dark holes of their eyes

continuous, eternal, wanting, weary

We look into our soul's smallest oasis,
the deepest wells of our hidden repentance.

# May Seung Jew

## WOMAN IN THE ROOM

Truth is a frequent visitor
to the woman in the room,
stares at her across the table,
stirring her tea with a spoon.
Stands beside her in the mirror,
with a knowing grin on his face,
as she fumbles here and fumbles there
with a nickel's worth of lace.
Truth speaks in tiny creaks
and muffled terms of endearment
as lying rigid in her bed she hears
lovers beyond the wall.

## SNOW

snow like the layers of these cool sheets

myself walking backwards along the long tunnel,
invoking.
the image and the echoes
emerge on cue
to disintegrate
like ashes.

the living fragments repeatedly lost,
richly on the verge of coalescence.

But at times
in a crowd under a hot sun
your arms finding me would not be unexpected,
assumed like the music,
and at times I find myself
hurrying to round a corner.


## WHEN I GET

when i get
to embrace
the wide horizons
of your shoulders

when i lie
sun-indolent
on your disputed plains

i sigh,
regretting
you too, prefer
some blinding moments in the sands
to fusion of our continents.

# LOVE SONG FROM A YOUNG LADY TO AN OLDER GENTLEMAN

my omniscient buddha
somnolent in the sun
regards the mystery of his navel
in profound meditation.

oh my celestial buddha
immobile as a rock
save when dreams of naked limbs
stir the sleeping rock.

I have seen our deity in underwear and socks.

when they genuflect before
another god,
and the cold rain pours
through your deserted shrine,
I will tend the broken rocks,
patient, chaste, and unconverted.

# Surjeet Kalsey

## VOICES OF THE DEAD

Fragile/ arrow/ this side up/
handle with care/ secret is secured/
safe in this black box/
the meaning of life is so brittle/
never thought/
humans and their flesh/blown in the air/
shredded so cruelly/ never thought of it/

Not even a thin veil/peel of an onion
was between life and death
it was/a vast devastating ocean/
from where throbbing starts/from where
stillness takes over/ there wasn't
any sign/any line in between/the wind
and the surging/surfing of the high waves/
. . . and what was/that moment/when
an ocean/ was dried up/within me/ I don't
know/ when the earth/was shattered '
within me/ I can recall the moment/when I
turned to a stone/ and many people after.

Countless faces, countless eyes
stopped at this shore/crossroads
of the ocean and the sky/ to find out
any clue of the 329 bodies/ shreds
metal scrap/ vanished in the
ocean within few moments. . .
WHY? WHAT FOR?

I forgot to breathe with many
slivers in my heart.
                    some maniac force
still saying:
whichever sound will voice the reason
whichever ear will hear the reason
whichever pen will print the reason
whichever eye will read the reason
will be handled with care/ will be
se/ver/ed with care!

Black box can keep the secret only
not the truth: before the blowout
all the people on board were alive/
the black box cannot bring them
back in flesh and blood, it cannot
bring back their breath.


## AGAINST THE WAVE

I was looking at the sunflowers
when the light turned to yellow-saffron
a signal to slow down or to rush up.
This is just a matter of an angle:
I know, people don't like moderates.
Still I don't want to rush up,
I will stay in the lane.

There was a flowing river of saffron
marigold flowers—a saffron crowd
rushing, hitting, running over or
being run over, restless, blindfolded
some feet stopped, some swept along,
some stunned, turned their faces backward,
toward the source of the wave and
started walking toward the opposite.

Wondering, who are they?
What are they who play with the people
and with their sentiments.
zzzzzzzzz . . . hush . . . hushshshshshshshsh
Nothing can stop the voices of the dead.

Would they be able
to touch the limits of the sky?
Would they be able
to promise us our life?
Would they bring us back our children,
our men, our fathers, our brothers, our
sons, our daughters; our mothers,
our wives, our sisters?
Would they be able to restore
the countless bodies?
Would they?
Would they!

What would they have to offer?
For the time being they can offer only
the red food color with smearing
as can dramatize their wounds
and become the martyrs.

Those of us who started walking toward
the other side of the wave do not even
qualify for this color.

# AN ECLIPSE

An eclipse of the moon,
That's what they called her
when she first entered the
threshold of his parents'
house, his house.

She was told she was Eve and
a part of Adam's flesh
she wondered then how could he—
strip her naked in front of his
blood relations. How?

Her soul was lying bare
on the cold floor, trying to
cover up with her beggar words
which were bouncing back at her body
like rocks
        rocks they were throwing at her.
By the time the moon went down
her soul her body her very existence
were all drenched with disgrace.

Over the years
they slashed her chip by chip,
very gently, to cut to the size
of their expectations.
They are very smart,
they know the art of taming
of a woman to make her
a harmless docile creature
by just placing her in the shoe
by putting her down, and calling her
an eclipse
        on their son, the moon.

## MISSING BASIS

Each morning
the first rays of the rising sun
reminds me how lonely was the night.
Two people must have some basis
to bear each other.
Some crowded moments of our
denying self, deny the other self.
Now we live very close to each other
like two parallel lines.
No basis. No memory
of the lost footprints.
                    There is void.
There is silence.
There is vast desert spread out
in front of our feet.
There is a feel of emptiness
and every moment reminds
a mirage of an oasis . . .
for eternal thirst.

Standing among the ruins, I can hear
the laughter of the statues echoing with
my voice, I found my head hanging from a
headless statue unsupported with his
stretched-out arms.

# Joy Kogawa

## FOR A BLANK BOOK

I have a peculiar
leaf shaped ears.
My fur is
forest colored.

When your flesh
first uttered words
I lost understanding.

You said I attend
stone and not flesh
source and not blood
bread and not bone—

your flesh
your blood
your bone—

which brings you to
mistrust of me.

And all the while
the stone bleeds
the source calls your name
the bread is broken,

but you cannot see
or hear
or taste.

Listen then, my love
to the wind blowing
and the sound of breath
over the grassy forest floor—

but know I did not bend
to the right or to the left
all the while
that I loved you.


## SHE HAS BEEN HERE FOR THREE MONTHS

She has been here for three months
silent as a saint on trial and
regal as a snow queen. Sometimes
with a sudden smiling grace, a
child's face, she moves through the
nursing home thick with
stammering woodpeckers in her
private popcorn tree country.

Gone from her familiar orchard
to a glacial whiteness she picks
with great delicacy the fruits
of her new winter trees.

Daily she waits for her
grandchild's letters—
sometimes on walker
sometimes in wheelchair.
She breathes the country odour
of last fall's hay
and watches the dandelions
growing white
and whiter and blowing finally
tiny umbrella puffs

across the open field.
And everywhere she sees
the earth bled to stubble—
dry as husks of hay
dry as egg shells.

It is time, dry time
all crying past.
It is time burning
burning in the air
and the small white
dandelion seedlings
are smoke trails showing
the pathway home.

## STATIONS OF ANGELS

Within the universe of flame
in the time between
watching and waiting
are the fire creatures
holy and unholy
hungry for those
many colored parts of us
which have no names.

Blow out the candle, friends
quickly, and let us
close our eyes
while the devouring
is at hand.

At the heart of our stillness, in
peaceable flames we shall
hear

shall we not hear
our mothers
singing.


## MINERALS FROM STONE

For many years
androgynous with truth
I moulded fact and fantasy
and where they met
made the crossroads home.

Here the house built
by lunatic limbs
fashioning what is not
into what might be—

a palace cave
for savage saints with
hunting knife still moist.

Bring me no longer
your spoils.
I have a house in the
shadows now and have
learned to eat minerals
straight from stone.

# ROAD BUILDING BY PICK AXE

*The Highway*

Driving down the
highway from Revelstoke—
the road built by
forced labour—all the
Nisei having no
choice etcetera etcetera
and mentioning this in
passing to this Englishman
who says when he
came to Canada from
England he wanted to
go to Vancouver too but
the quota for professors
was full so he was
forced to go to Toronto.


*Found Poem*

Uazusu Shoji
who was twice wounded
while fighting with the Princess Pats
in World War I
had purchased nineteen acres of land
under the Soldiers Settlement Act
and established a chicken farm.

His nineteen acres
a two-storied house
four chicken houses
an electric incubator
and 2,500 fowl
were sold for $1,492.59.

After certain deductions

for taxes and sundries were made
Mr Shoji received a cheque
for $39.32.


## The Day After

The day after Sato-sensei
received the Order of Canada
he told some of us Nisei
the honor he received
was our honor, our glory
our achievement.

And one Nisei remembered
the time Sensei went to Japan
met the emperor
and was given a rice cake
how Sensei brought it back to Vancouver
took the cake to a baker and
had it crushed into powder
so that each pupil might
receive a tiny bit.

And someone suggested
he take the Order of Canada medal
and grind it to bits
to share with us.


## Memento

Trapped in
a clear plastic
hockey-puck
paperweight
is a black ink sketch
of a jaunty outhouse.

Slocan Reunion—
August 31, 1974
Toronto.


*May 3, 1981*

I'm watching the flapping
green ferry flag on the
way to Victoria—
the white dogwood flower
centred by a yellow dot.

A small yellow dot
in a BC ferry boat—

In the Vancouver *Daily Province*
a headline today reads
"Western Canada Hatred
Due to Racism."

Ah my British
British Columbia, my
first brief home.


*For Issei in Nursing Homes*

Beneath the waiting
in the garden in
late autumn—how
the fruit falls without
a thud, the white
hoary hair falls and
falls and strangers
tread the grey walkways
of the concrete garden.

How without vegetation how
without touch the old ones

lie in their slow days.

With pick axe then
or dynamite

that in their last breaths, a
green leaf, yes, and
grandchild bringing gifts.

# Mina Kumar

## MIRA AWAITS KRISHNA IN RIVERSIDE PARK

When I wander down to the river banks,
it has just stopped raining. They say you come
with the rains. I walk the wet, leaf-slick paths
misled by the heavy bowing of trees,
the shifting of the wind, thinking I hear
music, your laughter, but it's only the
stereo of a passing car. Dusk falls;
the sky is turned the color of your skin.
They say at dusk you come. I wait;  a bird's
shivering shakes rain from branches. I walk
slowly the wet open paths to my home.
Another night no one will lift my gown.

## SANDHANA

Church bells and mango jelly sandwiches,
white socks and bic pens with the palest blue ink,
orange beads on metal wires counting out
one, ten, a hundred. Oh, the cube that was
a thousand, tempting me away from the
teacher's voice. I always got distracted
from the point. I even lost the relay
race bedazzled by the beaded baton.
What a little kindergarten loser
with my salad bowl haircut and plaid shirts.
My cousin, slick and older, taught me bad

words with patience as we lay in bed, light
from the party trickling under the door.
The adults thought they knew about risqué
with their pale drinks, Pakistani disco
and eau de cologne adultery, but
even her mother, that morose white rat, or
her wastrel father couldn't compare to my
cousin. Sent by our grandmother to
buy stamps, she taught me how much we could spend
on mitai pink mitais, sultry jujubes,
how many stamps we could pretend to have lost
on the way. I kept the sweets hidden in
my pillow case long after she went home;
red ants trickled over my cheek for days.


## THE HOUSE WAS DANK AND DEEP

The house was dank and deep. I ran through it
quickly in my clicking plastic shoes, to
the kitchen where my great-grandmother sat
against the faded orange saris hanging from the ceiling beams,

dripping. I ate the bananas she had mashed
and she gave me tin cups with which to play
as she had given my mother when Ma was six,
and she was already old. The others of the house

were old too and gray: my great-aunt who let me win
at dull games, drew elephants for me
each time I came; my grandfather clouded by
the dust of his files, motes settling

on his crabbed face. I sat behind his great desk when he wasn't there,
at the edge of a mottled sea of blotting paper,
reaching for his stout paperweights. My mother

was off in those lands in the glass:

wooden cabins, blonde children, snowmen. I set them back
on the desk and ran
through the cavernous house, my little voice echoing,
past the dusty veena splaying out its broken strings

that no one had tried to repair since the twin
great-aunts had succumbed to cholera,
up the dark stairs to the sudden,
golden roof where baby mangoes withered on straw mats

and my great-aunt gazed out upon the town,
quiet and quite sad. The sun set. If I had to stay
the night, I climbed up on my great-grandmother's bed,
and blanched like almonds in hot water

by my day, I lay in the shadow of her huge weight
and begged her the story of Prahalada, who
survived his father's hatred because
he had faith. Lulled a little by her voice,

swept by the shadows of the whirring
fan, I would pick at the green worms

on the back of her hand,
the single glistening hair on her chin.

My Aunt Jyo can't believe the dimness of my memory.
She says that I went willingly, happily.
That there's nothing to regret. I enjoyed myself.
They knew I was a child, that I loved them in a child's way.

# LEAVING

Taking the Via Rail she leaves town, watches the
landscape slide by, pulling easily, like hands
pulling a pail up from a well,
wheels squeaking and turning, spilling
water on the grass.

Outside, in the dim sunlight,
rotting yellow school buses crouch in dandelion fields,
their smashed windshields gaping maws
in midroar.

Without regret and with washed out memory, she thinks
of being young, a child in Scarborough,
the fields of concrete
outside the school, the red gouges on her knees.
She is leaving now, leaving being
the reason for black and white children to come together,
the scarred meeting ground quaking with
pushing and shoving and screaming, opening the red
scars of her please, please, PLEASE.

Outside, the sky is blue and willfully blind.

Without regret and with washed out memory, she thinks
of being young, a girl in Meadowvale,
the sparkling of her new
body, sparking evenings along the lake,
lazily spent on vinegar chips and popsicles,
watching the coming together of white bodies.
In the darkness, she was invisible.
She is leaving now, leaving being
the shadow of young desire, the dark purple
skin of red-fleshed plums.

Outside, the sun is setting behind electric trees
heavy with fat birds, glass insulators.

Without regret and with washed out memory, she thinks
of being a young woman in Richmond Hill,
washing the floors with a sponge amidst
the walk of mud-caked boots, on her knees
because they refused to buy a mop.

She was slapped and stinging from
the diamond on a white woman's finger. She curled up
sobbing to Billie Holiday on the radio,
because there was nowhere to crawl.
She is leaving now, leaving being
nothing more than surrender to the night, a black mynah bird
straining to peck at the stars.

Outside are huddled houses snapping open
with light.

She thinks without grief and opens the pages
of the place she is journeying toward. She is
leaning toward the caress
of low-fisted clouds.

Women behind her unwrap steaming, fragrant roti,
and it is stinging her eyes. She is leaving town, going to the
City, where night is filled with hot summer
noise and the rush of strangers. She is yearning for it,
longing for it, as she begins to cry.

# Carolyn Lei-lanilau

## ON THE DEATH OF GU CHENG

Boy in your silly hat
how thorns fit in your head so well!

Silly boy, little hat
dreams inside your eyes blinded
that you drank

Rainwater in the sweet nuts
water in the white sands or snow

Warm salt water for your little body
blue black water floats your heart anytime
(No need for kites or fire)

Dark avenues your wide red heart
snakes: your butterfly thoughts
*haidz!**

Sweat on your hot skin
rose petals, your cheeks
oyster and palms to eat day or night

Murderer of a woman who did not matter
boy, how could you not
build sandcastles?

Aunty Wind, Sun, Moon
Mother Earth: you loved inspite *dou zheng**
classic—"poet" "penniless" "exiled"

"Murderer" is what the Chinese name you:
hot gossip tastes delicious!
and what about the boy, your boy?

Today when I walk to market
wearing black and blue socks,
I ache from your voice

How I hope your soul is warm
by the sleep you often mummered
maybe Wilds will bless your hands.

If I might mighty boy, wish you peace in your
dream of everlasting
singing dancing eating
lovemaking
dreams and desiring
your lonely wife

Go to her man
beg in your Apollo voice
draw her gently in the small room with a slice of sky

Now: not try nothing*
now, Love
No more emperor-class measurements for man
or woman: no more similes of "cow" for Her

Be the light that landed once before you boy
no need to be the poet you hate
Pond full of lilies: you

You, bird on page sixty-eight of your *Selected Poems*
—stupid brother, don't look
you, the big cannon walking step by step

inside your heart: you mother you
No more Middle Kingdom
Beijing does not exist

Kiss your breath
touch her wounds
this is no opera

Shelve a roof in her mother's heart
offer pigs and ducks to her father's ancestors
soothe them now while you really can

As you boasted do!
"scatter amid the hacking"
"gather into her shadow on the surface of the water"*

And then what?
know for certain it is true:
your dreams are waking

Your wife: alive, bloody
you, snoring; belt around your neck
no one at your gate except your shadow sister

No one comes to reinvent you
no Chinese American quotes your wisdom
there is no mercy being a poet

You wrote that

*haidz:* kid, child
*dou zheng:* struggle session
*not try nothing: *wu bu wei*
* from *Overlapping Shadows* by Gu Zheng

## PARABLE

*For Ma*

(as luck would have it) Mother had no silver spoon
stuck in her stomach

sometimes when I'm talking to her on the phone
I'll say (as the conversation had been planned centuries ago
in another language) what did you eat (for lunch or dinner)?

sometimes she'll say she had a cup of tea for dinner
(and as the script reads) I'll say "a cup of tea!"
(which is the complex part of Chinese opera—tragic and comic
                                              simultaneously
while providing further discourse)

Mildred: my mother is magic
proof that you can be something from nothing
she is happy she is kind she is wise

at eighty-eight, she drives her 1978 Dodge sedan
to the mall, the cemetery and the temple
once in a while she forays to Las Vegas and
less frequently, she visits Oakland where her grandchildren grew up

during my last visit home to Hawaii, after loading me
      with provisions
she tied the box with string that she saved from Maunakea Street
from the heart of Chinatown and *lei* sellers
then she polished it off with a sturdy big red ribbon which waved
"aloha!    Aloha!" as it peeped up onto the mainland baggage claim

(who knows why?) I saved it
and today, Ana is flying back to Washington
for the remainder of her freshman year in college

(as scripture prophesies) she is taking back food and
*maybe* one book or apple blossoms and forget-me-nots from

the back yard
which she may allow me to force upon her

everything is in the suitcase or fortune cookie box from Chinatown

grandma's string will tie it all up and that red ribbon
(you can be sure) will be jumping and waving

"Ana! Aye Ana!
Kalea-Qyana, we're right here"

## HANGZHOU NEVER SO GOOD IN OAKLAND

*For Jacqueline Lokelani Lau*

Measuring sky by feet near the river
I smell gods
while water in the sun's breath hangs
heavy with groan.

But beneath the cassia and ancient magnolia,
watched by civilized stone gates, my imagination presses
        considering:
is it time to feed again?

Patches of jasmine and morning glory
distract my senses
(moment nursing summer).

Light in my skin; an average Chinese body not attached to earth.
Nipples swell inside my dress.
Juice brews within cadence of my one thigh rubbing

other.

I faint in a treasury of delight
as the street cracks and showering leaves demand attention.

Gods are so picky:
only like the best, usually the clever and kind.
Pretty doesn't count.
The lucky ones are obedient, scheme and ineligible:
gods don't eat slaves.
They want everything and expect nothing

which is why to be eaten by them
is such an honor.

## THE STRUCTURE OF BILL BLAKE WITHIN ME

*The Comment was "I really enjoyed reading your pieces. If you should develop a more structured non-fiction work, I hope you will let me have a look. Best of luck to you."*

1.
Darling sister
I understand everything Now.
It was through Mary Smith's prose that I discovered
pharaoh.
There: in polished English
phoenix posing so Mary and multicultural mom
could toast *sake* to the ancestors.
Plum blossoms sighed (as usual);
the sun deep in mediation.
Kicking through Acts I and II
empty (imitating White Buddha), I ordered text
in the tombs between silk and bamboo,

my sacred ears slipping in *haole* convention
consoled by civilized courtesy.
" 'Lyricism' baby" as you might quip.

Sister, we share a mother
but that *your* father's skin is the side of morning
and mine not
provides momentum in my bones and muscle
to lengthen and dig like virus.

How I crave to be a held chicken in a tapestry
my blond eyes confused in the night or
a bowling ball (pitched like a baseball)
in language that strangles sex and music.
Verbs and adjectives re-arranged,
nouns do not exist:
recreation, (re)creation, cereal is substance.


2.
What *is*
the value of
anything?

Cluster of apples, their leaves
now brittle huddle together
in a box destined from the backyard
to a city apartment.

My essays sail to unknown judges
through the same system as the apples.
Their separate but equal weight
costs the same:
can this be Right?
There is a Chinese artist.

There is another Chinese artist.
Both women paint like Christmas lights.
For five years, I couldn't talk to Liz.

Yesterday I saw her, her paintings.
Why is it I could weather double smiles
of Chinese women and avoid
the temptation of Lizzie's cosmogony?

It is a little like making love with
the wrong man: who *could* give you a house or a car or title.

Eventually, hands become air and bread
to paint the body an invented ritual

because spirit, its enzymes or chromosomes
are teeth grating, fists shooting
faint layers of apples and leaves
from childhood's heart.


3.
What next?

in our own zones
Liz
I:
the feet lower to
basement and greet Empress Menopause
who is attended by Persephone.


4.
Lei-aloha and I
pay big money to sing and laugh with each other on the
$$\text{telephone.}$$

"Why!"
screeched mother the husband and children

"Why?"
quacked lover lawyer the duck
"*Pourquoi?*" wooed the cow; "*wai wai*" rendered rooster

"why" weeped moss and sweet bunny rabbits
"Why" groaned rocks as mules beeped horns
Why? went the list
Y shrieked the cells
WHY cracked thunder threatened by waves

Why not! kisses rain on our hearts and toes:
merry is our innocence; divine, the experience

## HARRY'S CHINA

Harry's idea of China
includes white fish
hanging by their jaws in rows
above a woman's head as she
pounds millet in a junk.

Barely, the faces of
rooster and hen peek
through wood and wire.

The Great Wall
is background as
wife and sisters look proud
and shy every time
Harry said,
        "Smile."

My favorite is a movement with
vertical grey whitening boards
in the aqueduct: succession of
water windows reflecting
light climbing into a blur
of country sky.

Aunties wonder why I like the ulgies
while Harry
calm like all his China
hands me art
easy
as scooping up steamy rice.

# Wing Tek Lum

## ON M BUTTERFLY

The man who waits at the bus stop every night for his wife
    as an act of love
The man who bakes pastries the way they do in Hong Kong
    without much sugar
The man who drives a taxi with photos of his daughters
    propped on his dashboard
sees in movies
    the detective with his eyes made up
walking about on dainty feet

The man whose bookkeeping makes him a hero
    at the nursing home
The man who moonlights as a full time cook
    after his day at the supermarket
The man who applies lacquer with a Chinese brush
    to the furniture he has made
watches on television
    the faceless gangsters in pin stripe suits
lugging briefcases with opium and laundered money

The man who swears his daily tai chi exercise
    helps him sell insurance
The man who gave up golf for narcissus bulbs
    and has never regretted it
The man who always argues with his father at their store
    and then drives with him back home
follows on the stage
    a pale spy in flowing robes
dressed like a woman to deceive men

# AN IMAGE OF THE GOOD TIMES

It would be at dinner
when I was just a kid
when my brothers were away in college
and there were just three of us
around our small table in the kitchen
my mother sitting to my right
and my father to the right of her
—that is, sitting opposite me
with his back to our chopping block.
And we would be finishing our meal
our rice bowls empty
our chopsticks and spoons laid on our plates
the dishes on our lazy susan
waiting to be cleared.
And my father would turn to the bunsen burner
hooked up to a spigot by the counter.
In a stainless steel pot
he would bring water to a boil.
In turn the water would be poured
into a small clay pot
he had stuffed full of his favorite leaves.
While waiting for his tea to brew
he would raise his leg
resting its heel against the edge of his chair
his thigh tucked into his chest.
He would reach over
underarm supported by his knee
to pour the tea into his cup.
The cup, saucer and pot were a matching set
and we learned over the years
never to wash them
to add to the dark pungency.
He would finish off the tea
in large, measured gulps
smacking his lips at the end
with a loud sigh of satisfaction
as if it could echo

against the chaos of the world
that reigned outside our home
outside of that love that bound us together
through our bad times and all the good.

## THE DEVOUT CHRISTIAN

I am driving back
to my eldest brother's place
with the roast pig in my trunk
feeling relieved and proud
having just finished our *baai saan*.
We had laid the annual pig
in front of the tombstones
along with our full plates
of fish and shrimp, chicken and duck,
spooned out our rice,
poured cups of tea
and some very old whiskey.
We stood solemn before our ancestors
moving our clasped hands up and down.
We lit red candles and incense,
set off packs of firecrackers
and burned colored paper
as currency for our dead.
And as I approach a stoplight
I reflect on how each year
we pay homage to six of them like this.
And suddenly the thought comes to me
like some of that crumpled paper
bursting into bright flame.
In the hustle and bustle of this morning
we forgot to offer a silent prayer
to our seventh one buried there,
to my mother, the devout Christian,
who had told us never to worship her

as if like those others
her spirit were still alive.
I drive on keeping the neglect to myself
as I discuss with my wife
how I will later on
have to rush our daughter
to her piano lesson.
I leave it like that
forgetting the guilt
of forgetting my mother
as if such burnt out ashes
could be simply swept away
by the wind and water of these mountains.
To my brother's kitchen
I go about helping my sister-in-law
chop up the whole pig
on a block I recall my father got
from the trunk of a tamarind tree.
We wash up the dishes
and pack the leftovers
into plastic bags to freeze.
As we are about to go
my daughter and I put on our shoes
near the steps to the sitting room.
There she remembers
the large photos of my parents
and the one of my mother
with her face slightly tilted to one side,
her gray hair going white,
her smile exposing
that gap between her front teeth
like a darkness that will not go away.
My daughter says
that when she came into the house
she forgot to *ching ching*
in front of them as she usually does.
But somehow today is special
and she tells me
she wants to say a prayer to her.

She walks over to the photo
and in a shy voice
sings a song in Hawaiian
that she learned from school
—what she says for grace
before eating lunch.
Like the stillness after firecrackers
I try to hold back my surprise.
Calming myself I ask her why
she wanted to do what she just did.
She remembers that I once told her
that *poh poh* liked to pray.
How in sweet heaven
she thought of all of this
on this very morning,
so bright and clear, is a wonder.
I do not know
and I do not dare to ask.
I hug her tightly and tell her
how proud I am of her.
It is enough as always.
Like our graves swept clean of weeds
I know now all is forgiven.

# Bhargavi C Mandava

## HEARING TONGUES

Listen for the chandelier
crushed by a galloping horse,
as the rain patters on
sleeping shingles.
A child stands under the
shelter of a window sill,
peeling back the golden foil
sheathing an expensive chocolate.
The sound of shhhh from
the rustling of skin on skin
of starved lovers, who pause
for a breath when they
hear the tinkling of
pine needles falling on ice
and icicles falling on pine.
A child hits the shrillest key
on a toy piano again and again,
but fails to awaken
his father who is snoring
with a broken neck.
The clink of an earring
against a bone and
the scraping of a beard
against a nipple: all the while,
a grave is being dug nearby,
where you can hear a
seedling break through cement,
if you listen. It is two dogs
playing with a hat;

it is anise tea filling clay;
it is a pencil tip catching
on the fiber of paper;
it is Agni's tresses blowing
forward and backward;
it is all this,
this trembling fire before me.
Before me, it is I, trembling.

## INDIAN FEVER

Grandmother's silver toe-rings, wedding
presents, clinked on the stone floor—
the sound of porcelain cups resting
on saucers. But there was no tea there.

Mother was in her feverish belly,
patiently waiting to wage war beside her;
To tell the frightened strangers that we
are all petals of the same flower.

Grandfather was snoring in a nearby
jail cell, chill and darkness conquered like
British sensibility. He was fluent in seven
languages. And his wife? Only one.

Six others (one died of diphtheria)
followed Mother, who was soon helping
Grandmother cook for the hundreds
who came knocking at their house

During the monsoons. It was then that
Mother first touched the untouchables and
began to see her purpose. When Gandhi
was shot, everyone cried—even the children.

Mother was the only one to study.
As a doctor, she ran a free clinic and
knocked on palm huts to give away
contraceptives. But Father had an itch.

In 1972, Mother asked the stewardess
for something—anything vegetarian.
She gave her a red apple the size of a
mango. We shared it. We didn't recognize

Father at JFK airport. He was so fat. He asked
us if it was hot in India and we didn't answer.
Then, something about the lemon pickle jars
leaking fiery orange oil. He missed home.

In 1978, we started eating Big Macs and I
started my period. Mother yelled when she
discovered the blood in the wastepail.
If we were in India . . .

If we were in India, they'd have a big
celebration. They would make sweets
of sesame and brown sugar and pour
sweet milk in my mouth for fertility.

I decided yesterday that I don't want
a baby right now. I've killed cacti from
neglect. I don't have time to read or
cook even. What do you do with all the

Day and night, she asks. And I cannot
answer. I've copied some recipes, but
she doesn't use a measure. How? She just
knows. When I ask her how to make tea—

Chai? She laughs and laughs. Indian tea.
It's so easy. She says to ask her about
more complicated dishes like idli or dosai
and that, soon, I won't have anyone to ask.

Like malaria the words catch, setting me on
fire like Father burning in that cheap casket
somewhere on Long Island; catching like our
house with the swimming pool no one used.

How silly I stand holding a cold torch,
trying to peel my brown-brown skin and
yank out this long black hairnoose—
how silly until Mother starts telling stories

That start smoldering like heaps of
sugar-cane roots on rural roadsides;
they're making way for the new life-shoots;
and beyond the smoke, an iceblue sky.


## ABSENCE

the blood in my heart bursts
like two crowflocks colliding
and scattering through the
whitest cloudfeet of heaven,
and, here, truth's black claws
slap my cheeks; I have been told.
the studio smells of decay,
of last month's flowers and
my morning bagel—onion;
your canvases have hollow stares;
paint stale on palette and
brushes stiff like forgotten limbs.
the awful silence in the rooms:
your cool pillow covered
by my hair and a library book
about psychology; the usual tree
trembling with shrieks of swallows
at sunset and again at sunrise;
oh, the stillness in these sheets—

the blood in my heart bursts
like two crowflocks colliding
and scattering through the
whitest cloudfeet of heaven,
and, here, truth's black claws
shred my chest; I am branded.


## MOONSWEETS

The guava tree shimmers
as a parrot cleans its green face.
She stares straight ahead
as if rudraksha beads were passing
beneath her thumb, but
she is not meditating—
she is cooking.
Once the scent of sesame and
brown sugar on her fingers
from rolling sweet butterballs
smelled of jasmine buds.
She does not wear flowers in her hair
since her husband died.
It is a breezy afternoon sounding of
rickshaw bells and wet saris
striking laundry stones in backyards.
Her granddaughter scampers down
the garden walkway, screaming news.
Her small, perfect fingers tuck
a hibiscus blossom behind
her Ammamma's ear.
The woman looks at herself rippling
in the cask of dark water,
amidst fallen leaves and mosquitoes.
"I'm hungry," says the girl
because she is growing,
so Ammamma shakes out her hands and

wipes them on her widow-white sari.
Through the gauze and sun, her arms and
feet seem to disappear; she is half ghost.
As she walks to the cupboard, the
hibiscus slips, leaving a comet trail
of vermilion at her back.
Her granddaughter does not notice
as she eyes the silver canister
brimming with pale full-moons.


## DESERT HAIKU

Tortoise marches toward
creosote's shade
belly to belly
yellow blooms.

Whir of hummingbirds
crazed by the silent bursting
of April rockets.

Plump moths twirling
spilling dust;
yellow buds
yellow moon
yellowyellow.

Ocotillo fingertips
scrape jagged blue,
bleeding into blossoms.

Crushed sand pearls cling to
tortoise claws and fuschia lips
awaiting spring's kiss.

Caught in purple caught
in petal caught in cactus
caught in desert caught.

Desert sun hammers
breaking open bitter green
seedless scarlet melon.

Weary limbs unfolding
grandfathers' wooden lap.
Trees, delightful trees.

Cholla frames velvet
sand streams where a lizard sits,
watching the sky change.

The smell of silver
oasis-drop shatters on
breast stripped by wild clouds.

Orange sunslices
slip onto a sable snake
sunning on a rock.

Two lovers nuzzling
into the pink
slumping neck
of the drowsy sun.

Glimpse orange fishtail
splash behind bluish mountain;
sunset missed again.

With sun asleep and
crescent moon nestled in bed,
shooting stars collide.

A flower brushes
stone shoulders; desert lovers

illumed by moonsparks.

The open mouth of
silence
til the sudden whoosh
of a jack rabbit.

The open arms of
elders and Joshua trees
patiently waiting.

# David Mura

## THE YOUNG ASIAN WOMEN

The young Asian women are shaving their heads,
piercing eyelids and ears. They find themselves staring
at a meteor shower walking round lakes
on January nights when the ice crackles
and pops like bubble gum in their jaws.
Their names are Juliana, Vong, Lee and Lily.
She could be Mina from the outskirts of Tokyo
but more likely she is N'kaulis of the famous
or infamous Lyfongs (depending on your clan
and your anti-Communist persuasions). She
could be some siren named Sophia too in love
with her looks, a nasty sense of indiscretion in her
smile. And if her name is Hoa, she's tough
as her mother, a tough cookie, bad girl, bitch,
it doesn't matter, she'll survive like nettles,
flower in what ditch she finds herself, with
or without a man, or her lesbian lover who left
for Alaska, the smell of bearshit on the trail.
With her Taiwanese aunt, digs tales of Toisan
ladies, dragons and the water marsh where bandit
ghosts steal your years with a kiss, talking
tongues down your throat to your belly, slipping
a demon seed inside you to grow. Oh, they
are like that, these young women, their art alive
like a razor on your cheek, like the hurtling of hooves
or a half pint of bourbon lying on the nightstand;
they know how mysteriously the body is written,
how the thundering colors of Bennetton befit
the statistics of garment workers in the Third

and First Worlds. They know Woman Warrior,
bell hooks, how the moon waxes red like the sheet
of paper where they write out their scripts, stories
and poems, unwrapping their dreams before you
like a fistful of pins, dust, pearls, sweat and stones.
Their boots are black and buckled, their jeans frayed,
their lips bruised purple or incandescent red,
and on the dance floor their bodies catch hip-hop
like a sail seizes breeze, bobbing, weaving and wild.
Their voices are hoarse after a night on the floor,
their faces smeared with sweat. Their cheeks glow.
They scare the pants off the young men they know.

## THE WORDS ON MY TONGUE

I am nine, sitting in a circle with our teacher.
I am to read out loud. Though I know these words
—*ball, the, I, throw, boy, girl*—they lodge
in my throat, dry as cotton balls, a cough that won't leave.
My teacher wears a look of concern or impatience,
it doesn't matter. My classmates giggle or shift
in boredom, it doesn't matter. The words
lie like ammunition on the page. I will not fire them.
(The gun aims at the centre of my chest.)
The minutes pass, the day is long. Finally,
the teacher asks the next student to read on.

Deep at night, that first winter,
I lay in the cupola
of my sheets and rubbed
my hands together, half
in prayer, half
like two sticks, praying for fire.
Like those who took us in
as sponsors on Sunday,
I was asking for the Holy Spirit

to enter me, to speak in tongues of flame.

We were Chinese, from Sadec, just outside Saigon.
There the river flooded through the delta,
a miracle of mud and substances abounding
in the current—crates, chairs, water buffalo, branches
and sometimes bodies, the drowned
ones, eyes turned towards some other world.
My brother almost drowned there once.
My mother slapped me for taking him down.
That sting still rings in my ear like a gong.

I knew I spoke with this accent.
It was visible as a hump
or the limp my sister walks with,
the metal braces that reverberate her steps.
The noise that emptied from my mouth
contained a color I could not eradicate,
a grating sing song
like horsehair of a violin, a Chinese violin,
and even as I opened my mouth
I could see, in the eyes of a listener,
if they were white, spreading in every direction
across their face, a judgement
as inevitable as at evening
comes the descending night.

Uncomely noise, ugly noise, ching-chong
Chinamen noise, cavity ridden
and sounding of brown gums, yellowed teeth,
contorted lips struggling like some ape to speak,
and unlike the splinter
father drew with delicacy from my palm,
removing a pain I'd lived with all day,
down the streets of the city, the graffiti and traffic,
there was nothing he could do,
nor my mother. The words sat
on my tongue, like the questions
that sat inside my ear—*What did you say? What did he say?*

And yet,
even then, I was moving away,
coming to the time
when I would stand with father, mother,
before my teacher
and translate to them
both the praise, which I embellished,
and the checks, which I altered, fights
on the asphalt schoolyard of broken glass
and a rumbling in my stomach
that spoke incessantly of fear.
Deep in the magical jungle,
in some country we travelled
to, my parents were wandering,
and I had to lead them, word by word,
in the grocer's, before the lawyer, my teacher,
to meaning, sweet land of comprehension
rising like an island from the chaos of oceans
back in the beginning when God made the word and the world.

You children, you who take your foreign parents
into these unfamiliar streets
know this trembling, this fear;
and even though you speak *for* them,
you cannot speak your fear.

So what is it I do now in the corporation?
I open my eyes to numbers, their possible blossoming,
beauty comprehensible to my tongue,
and only those occasional afternoons,
speaking under fluorescence,
like a prisoner confessing the sins of a previous regime,
does it come back in the faces before me—

The smirk in their smiles, the sliver on my tongue.

And I know then
I have bitten

a ceiling of glass
which will never shatter
with the words I speak to you now
so like the words I spoke as a child

once upon a time, long ago: *Boy, ball, throw, me.*


## FATHER BLUES FOR JON JONG

Way back in the fifties
    when a Chinaman was a chink
        and chance a Chinaman's dance,
and Charlie Chan was still
    a wry mocking memory in the cinema
        of blue-eyed blondes;
when white boys were singing blues
    and angel headed hipsters
        coked and toked their dreams
on the road, in Beat Bay cafes
    back when Chinatown
        was full of Flower Drum Song—
Well, once in that glorious decade,
    my father was rising, PhD
        in chemistry, crashing
glass ceilings of Fluor Corporation
    with brains and acumen
        and easygoing laugh,
and like any white blueblooded American in the time
    of Leave It To Beaver, Donna Reed,
        and Father Knows Best,
father wanted to buy a house,
    and he didn't give a shit
        about Paladin and Hey Boy, Pa
Cartwright and Hop Sing,
    or Peter the cranky houseboy
        who kept Bachelor Father and Kelly

all clean and bright, like Cheer or All, so gleaming white;
        forget all those Stepan Fetchit
            chinky figures of fun, Ba-ba
was going to buy a house, come hell or highwater,
        and so he made bids on house after
            house all across this city,
and after every bid Ba-ba was told
        politely—or impolitely, it didn't really matter—Solly!
            Charlie Chinaman,
you don't have a chance!
        even if your offer rises higher the price,
            even if you send the price soaring
like the homers of the Say Hey
        Kid blasting over the fence,
            no way, Jose, NO WAY !
—But father was never a man to take no,
        he asked a white friend to bid on a house, higher
            than the asking,
and his proxy bought the house,
        taking a commission on the side,
            and there we were living high on the hog
on a hill over Chinatown and the Bay,
        and father headed for Vice President, better salaries,
            bigger cars, the whole shebang . . .

And then. And then: SLAM—HEADLINE:
        June 29,1956, *New York Times:*
            126 Die in Plane Crash
down the Grand Canyon, the
        decade's largest disaster, larger
            than any other for me
with my father aboard, Ba-ba's
        remains mangled beyond
            recognition in the crumpling
and crush of metal, pyres of high octane
        flames, and Woo's Funeral Parlour
            in Chinatown serviced what was left,
and inside Woo's roaring oven,
        a small stellar holocaust

seared my father
down to a vase of ash, placed
    inside a lacquered wooden box,
        and my mother, three months
pregnant, hauled it
        to be buried in the Glendale Cemetery,
            her other arm tugging along, barely
two, a toddler teetering out of the Chevy,
    half conscious
            something was now amiss, amid
the rolling lawns and slabs of stone
        and the office where my mother stood, waiting
            for them to place what was left
of my father in a vault,
        and I don't know why, don't
            understand, my mother
is crying, is screaming, is yanking
        me out of that office, cursing in Chinese
            the white man behind the desk,
and only years later do I learn my father
        couldn't be buried there once
            they saw my mother, once
they saw her eyes, her skin, her
        lithe dark figure, her eyes, her skin
            in the boy beside her,
and the moral is, I suppose,
        one I've carted to this day—
            "It don't matter if you're burnt
down to ash, just primal dust,
        you still a Chinaman, you might as well
            play your life, your music that way

—Oh Chinaman Chinaman Chinaman blues . . ."

David Mura

# A CALIBAN'S CURSE

"You taught me language; and my profit on't
Is, I know how to curse. . ."

Oh Mr Motto Fu Manchu
Kung Fu ninja chopping you
Charlie Chan
chink and jap man

houseboy gardener laundry coolie
Miss Saigon's chop-chop suey
this is how our balls were banned
this is where they played our parts

fuck their yellow minstrel farce
fuck them in their white white hearts
fuck them till they fall apart
weeping for their white white art

# IN AMERICA

The season of searing Santa Annas,
brush fires that flare all night in the hills, taut
vibrant emanations of light, *ojiisan*

would drive them to the Pacific, just before
sundown and the long steaming L.A. night.
In that silver Packard reeking of cigar,

the children laughed and shouted, sang with him,
never understanding the words, China
nights, a soldier somewhere in Asia, swimming

in his solitude, the girl from home. Soon
he shuttled them out beneath the night sky,

and he talked on the beach of his boyhood

in Shingu, his father, going back to Japan
for *omiyai*, their mother. Told them again
they'd been born here, this was their homeland,

but someday he'd go back to die, rich as an emperor.
Nonsense, says his wife, as they clamber back,
and he opens the door like a chauffeur,

tipping his cap. The children giggle. And none
of them knows this life is condemned,
even as they fall asleep to his humming,

syllables that flash and vanish in their dreams
years later in Chicago, Stamford, Miami,
cities of their small diaspora. They wake, groping,

to find the song vanished, a faint wind searing
their faces, still scented with sea, cigar smoke,
this sadness they cannot name. And each hears

only the breathing of a companion, blue
shadows of morning betraying a normalcy
none of them imagines, sleeping in the back

of a Packard in 1930, '36 or '40.
These are the years of expectation, elation,
when he is unbroken, she not yet dreaming,

as in the fall of '41, of flames soaring,
exploding off the sea, some divine wind
raining damnation, disintegration, war.

Years in America when my father was a boy.
When my father was a Jap. In America.

# Suniti Namjoshi

## GRAVEN IMAGES

*For friends who asked me whether the gods I worshipped*
*were made out of flesh or made out of stone.*

1.
First, the squat minotaur, the toad
monster. He weighs 2 tons. He is made
out of stone. He has grown so heavy,
so extremely strong, that he cannot move.
You could run about naked. You could tickle
his nose. If he could lift his paw,
he'd probably kill,
                        but you're probably safe.
He cannot move. Caress his flanks,
the idol, the constant one.
                        And this is his wife,
also of stone. She loves no one.


2.
My idol, my pretty one, weep stone
tears, no one is watching.
They will think they are pebbles.
Every night his godship recedes, inches
into rock in the wind and rain.
It will probably take him 6,000 years,
7,000 years, to alter his smile,
to erode his nose. Human beings
help, their stroking and petting,
their persistent kissing.

His priests rub him down
in butter every day.


3.

Consider next, if you will, what the embrace of Pygmalion
must have felt like at first: he, human and sweating, she,
cold to the bone. He woke her with a kiss—under sun,
moon and stars, all of them at once and none competing?
His love awakened her? Kindled her to life? Have it your
way. It may be so. But consider also her mute anguish,
the effort required, and the pain it must have cost. They
loved one another: she, this marble man, he, this human
woman. But he was a sculptor. He carved another stone,
and she ran away with the man next door, who, as it
happened, was a potter and worked in mud.


4.

Under a stone tree of which
the leaves are made of stone,
a man lies asleep. Even his lashes
are made of stone. Sometimes
an ant will cross an eyelid.
No muscle moves. This is a man
who was probably loved and thus preserved.


5.
"And what's her history?
A blank, my lord." *Twelfth Night* II, iv.

The suns slip past,
in the daylight one is tired,
but do not weep. As you sit
very still and turn into stone,
envy no one,
     not the girl made of grass,
     nor the girl made of straw.

You have your dignity, but their laughter
and delight can offend none.


## MINIMAL MURDER

He's coming through the grass to have a picnic. He has smooth
blue eyes with spiders in them. We spread out lunch and begin to
eat. I'm distracted by spider webs. These cling to my face, my
arms and knees. I brush them away, and we drink wine. The
spiders attack. I kill a few spiders. The food is littered with thou-
sands of insect tracks.

Thinking it over it seems to me that of the varieties of murder
insecticide coupled with clear self-defence may possibly be the
least heinous. But one must be cautious. There's a sect of Jain
monks who wear surgical masks and clear a space for themselves
with long-handled brooms before so much as venturing a step.
Do they feel anything? (I feel nothing.) Perhaps they exercise a
compassionate intellect.


## BIPED

Now that you have hit me,
        I must dab at my mouth
and smile quietly,
        or not smile at all,
but in some way show
        I am noble, not base.
And the dog inside,
        who whimpers
so piteously,
        and would like to lick your hands
—it feels so out of favor—

that dog must be silenced
before its howling
betrays disgrace.
But I am that dog.
It was I who howled,
I who was hurt.
I felt the pain.
And it is I
who despised myself.


## THE CREATURE

I was in the garden, at the edge
of a wood.
I knew she would come, the light
gliding
across her shoulder blades, down
her back,
her eyes reflecting the surrounding green.
I crept a little closer.
I think she saw me.
I came out of the bushes
and stared at her.
She seemed to be pleased.
She settled on the grass,
leaning her back against a tree trunk.
I knew she was waiting.
When she stretched out an arm,
I let her touch me.
I licked her throat, I cropped the grass
between her feet.
But then he appeared.
She looked up and laughed.
He looked down and smiled—
from a monstrous height.
I skittered off fast.

Then I came back
                    and watched them at it.

## THE FUR SEALS AS SHOWN ON TELEVISION

A female of the species has strayed
          too far. Beachmaster bellows
and staggers after her.
                              Rolls of fat
move oilily. I would like
                              to laugh,
but I hold my breath
              and wait for what follows.
Can't the female run?
                    Perhaps the female
does not wish to run?
                    The announcer says
"The male of the species
              is four times as large
but females are seldom
                    if ever, hurt.
Beachmaster hits her.
                    It's a blow
to the head.
              (She has such a sleek
and beautiful head.)
                    She goes down.
With a casual flipper
          he stows her underarm
and hauls her away.
                    The rest is not shown.

Another long shot,
              another beachmaster:
this one's beach
              is covered with water.

"But nothing deters him."
                    Proof is offered.
He grabs a female.
                    There's a noisy scuffle,
and a sleek head
                    forced underwater.
The TV announcer
                    is very excited.
I feel bruised. My head
                    hurts.

# Michael Ondaatje

## USWETAKEIYAWA

Uswetakeiyawa. The night mile

through the village of tall
thorn leaf fences
sudden odors
which pour through windows of the jeep.

We see nothing, just
the grey silver of the Dutch canal
where bright colored boats
lap like masks in the night
their alphabets lost in the dark.

No sight but the imagination's
story behind each smell
or now and then a white sarong
pumping its legs on a bicycle
like a moth in the headlights

    and the dogs
who lean out of night
strolling the road
with eyes of sapphire
and hideous body
      so mongrelled
they seem to have woken
to find themselves tricked
into outrageous transformations,
one with the spine of a snake
one with a creature in its mouth

(car lights rouse them
from the purity of darkness)
one that could be a pig
slaughtered lolling
on the carrier of a bike.

This is the dream journey
we travel most nights
returning from Colombo.
A landscape nightmare
unphotographed country.
The road hugs the canal
the canal every mile
puts an arm into the sea.

In daylight women bathe
waist deep beside the road
utterly still as I drive past
their diya reddha cloth
tied under their arms.
Brief sentences of women
lean men with soapy buttocks
their arms stretching up
to pour water over themselves,
or the ancient man in spectacles
crossing the canal
only his head visible
pulling something we cannot see
in the water behind him.
The women surface
bodies the color of shadow
wet bright cloth
the skin of a mermaid.

In the silence of the night drive
you hear ocean you swallow odors
which change each minute—dried fish
swamp   toddy   a variety of curries
and something we have never been able to recognize.

There is just this thick air
and the aura of dogs
in trickster skin.

Once in the night we saw
something slip into the canal.
There was then the odor we did not recognize.
The smell of a dog losing its shape.

## SWEET LIKE A CROW

*For Hetti Corea, 8 years old*

"The Sinhalese are beyond a doubt one of the least musical people
in the world. It would be quite impossible to have less sense of
pitch, line, or rhythm."
                    PAUL BOWLES

Your voice sounds like a scorpion bring pushed
through a glass tube
like someone has just trod on a peacock
like wind howling in a coconut
like a rusty bible, like someone pulling barbed wire
across a stone courtyard, like a pig drowning,
a vattacka being fried
a bone shaking hands
a frog singing at Carnegie Hall.
Like a crow swimming in milk,
like a nose being hit by a mango
like the crowd at the Royal-Thomian match,
a womb full of twins, a pariah dog
with a magpie in its mouth
like the midnight jet from Casablanca
like Air Pakistan curry,
a typewriter on fire, like a spirit in the gas
which cooks your dinner, like a hundred

pappadans being crunched, like someone
uselessly trying to light 3 Roses matches in a dark room,
the clicking sound of a reef when you put your head into
     the sea,
a dolphin reciting epic poetry to a sleepy audience,
the sound of a fan when someone throws brinjals at it,
like pineapples being sliced in the Pettah market
like betel juice hitting a butterfly in midair
like a whole village running naked onto the street
and tearing their sarongs, like an angry family
pushing a jeep out of the mud, like dirt on the needle,
like 8 sharks being carried on the back of a bicycle
like 3 old ladies locked in the lavatory
like the sound I heard when having an afternoon sleep
and someone walked through my room in ankle bracelets.


## THE HOUR OF COWDUST

It is the hour we move small
in the last possibilities of light

now the sky opens its blue vault

I thought this hour belonged to my children
bringing cows home
bored by duty swinging a stick,
but this focus of dusk out of dust
is everywhere—here by the Nile
the boats wheeling
like massive half-drowned birds
and I gaze at water that dreams
dust off my tongue,
in this country your mouth
feels the way your shoes look

Everything is reducing itself to shape

Lack of light cools your shirt
men step from barbershops
their skin alive to the air.
All day
dust covered granite hills
and now
suddenly the Nile is flesh
an arm on a bed

In Indian miniatures
I cannot quite remember
what this hour means
—people were small,
animals represented
simply by dust
they stamped into the air.
All I recall of commentaries
are abrupt lovely sentences where
the color of a bowl
a left foot stepping on a lotus
symbolized separation.
Or stories of gods
creating such beautiful women
they themselves burned in passion
and were reduced to ash.
Women confided to pet parrots
solitary men dreamed into the conch.
So many
graciously humiliated
by the distance of rivers

The boat turns languid
under the hunched passenger
sails
ready for the moon
fill like a lung

there is no longer
depth of perception
it is now possible
for the outline of two boats
to collide silently

# LIGHT

*For Doris Gratiaen*

Midnight storm. Trees walking off across the fields in fury
naked in the spark of lightning.
I sit on the white porch on the brown hanging cane chair
coffee in my hand midnight storm midsummer night.
The past, friends and family, drift into the rain shower.
Those relatives in my favorite slides
re-shot from old minute photographs so they now stand
complex ambiguous grainy on my wall.

This is my Uncle who turned up to his marriage
on an elephant. He was a chaplain.
This shy-looking man in the light jacket and tie was infamous,
when he went drinking he took the long blonde beautiful hair
of his wife and put one end in the cupboard and locked it
leaving her tethered in an armchair.
He was terrified of her possible adultery
and this way died peaceful happy to the end.
My Grandmother, who went to a dance in a muslin dress
with fireflies captured and embedded in the cloth, shining
and witty. This calm beautiful face
organized wild acts in the tropics.
She hid the mailman in her house
after he had committed murder and at the trial
was thrown out of the court for making jokes at the judge.
Her son became a QC.
This is my brother at 6. With his cousin and his sister

and Pam de Voss who fell on a penknife and lost her eye.
My Aunt Christie. She knew Harold MacMillan was a spy
communicating with her through pictures in the newspapers.
Every picture she believed asked her to forgive him,
his hound eyes pleading.

Her husband Uncle Fitzroy a doctor in Ceylon had a memory
sharp as scalpels into his 80s
though I never bothered to ask him about anything
—interested then more in the latest recordings of Bobby Darin.

And this is my Mother with her brother Noel in fancy dress.
They are 7 and 8 years old, a hand-colored photograph,
it is the earliest picture I have. The one I love most.
A picture of my kids at Halloween
has the same contact and laughter.
My Uncle dying at 68, and my Mother a year later dying at 68.
She told me about his death and the day he died
his eyes clearing out of illness as if seeing
right through the room the hospital and she said
he saw something so clear and good his whole body
for a moment became youthful and she remembered
when she sewed badges on his trackshirts.
Her voice joyous in telling me this, her face light and clear.
(My firefly Grandmother also dying at 68).

These are the fragments I have of them, tonight
in this storm, the dogs restless on the porch.
They were all laughing, crazy, and vivid in their prime.
At a party my drunk Father
tried to explain a complex operation on chickens
and managed to kill them all in the process, the guests
having dinner an hour later while my Father slept
and the kids watched the servants clean up the litter
of beaks and feathers on the lawn.

These are their fragments, all I remember,
wanting more knowledge of them. In the mirror and in my kids
I see them in my flesh. Wherever we are

they parade in my brain and the expanding stories
connect to the grey grainy pictures on the wall,
as they hold their drinks or 20 years later
hold grandchildren, pose with favorite dogs,
coming through the light, the electricity, which the storm
destroyed an hour ago, a tree going down by the highway
so that now inside the kids play dominoes by candlelight
and out here the thick rain static the spark of my match
                                                    to a cigarette
and the trees across the fields leaving me, distinct
lonely in their own knife scars and cow-chewed bark
frozen in the jagged light as if snapped in their run
the branch arms waving to what was a second ago the dark sky
when in truth like me they haven't moved.
Haven't moved an inch from me.

# S Padmanab

## CAMEL BY THE PERCOLATOR

how this house has grown,
fashioning the fields around it,
the white flower, wind-broken twig
and last winter's frayed, discolored leaves,
all in their impeccable places.

we have added rooms and drapes,
doghouse and dock,
and a boat for the water to lap against
(water should have a purpose
beyond common use).
and of course the children:
fingers soft and trusting,
snails in their pockets
or ladybugs in matchboxes.

but no, let me begin at the beginning,
if there is such a thing.
history is enormous.
we are all born too soon,
chiselled and sculpted
but never enough honed
for the times and places
we find ourselves in.

therefore this beginning too is tentative,
unsure of its end.
o yes, i was talking of the house and fields.
one day the camel driver brought the desert

to the edges of our lives.
he brought a dry, desiccated sun,
his mud-plastered beasts,
and a toothless grace.
i did not believe his story.
not then, not now.
but nothing is totally false.
perhaps there was a colored tent and a stolen wife,
silent but strong as a weathered tree.
her branches covered his life like a canopy,
and he had his decade of love and fulfilment
and the daughter of his desert heat
was gifted to me.

was this the story told by him?
or have i conjured this up?
what is my desire's pith
and what memory crusts my waking hours?
i have spent my years
defining the nape of your neck,
the flex of your wrist,
the swirl of your lips
and the whorls of your mind.
i have peeled, onion-like
(pale fruit without centre, contained nothingness,
transformed hide, the red of my restless sleep):
only to find that you are somewhere else,
within,
deeper yet,
where perhaps i can begin again.

coffee smell. turning of sheets
knife slicing the eggplant, striking its thunder
against the cutting board.
hum of dishwasher
domesticity defined by a percolator.

you lean away for a hurried kiss.
stay away! what damage you have done!

you have begun the cycle
and i must again analyze,
the black of your eye
the descent of hair
and the press of your body
against mine.

love, keep away.
this morning is dangerous, this moment too risky,
our children lost to bandanas, love beads,
pointed slippers, all-night parties
and piled-up books.
our children carried off our past.

so we are left with this:
sunday in the kitchen,
i alone with the fictitious daughter
stolen by a camel thief
with a fabricated past
(i must go away for a night, he said,
there is a place where brooms sell cheap.
i will be back tomorrow for my child,
my heartbeat and my talisman).

i know you do not believe this story:
there can be no housewife in north america
(with canada a.m. news, curlers and homo milk)
born to a camel thief.
you are perhaps right, logic has its place,
and its limitations

but how else did i become the lover
whose coming you did not see?
i have always been in your life, you say.
how else can i explain this morning
when the willow sings
and the river flows by,
oblivious of the tales we tell?

each one must have a destiny.
mine is to invent tales, this or another,
truthful or improbable,
till i find the one that fits
the hollows of your hands,
the spaces between your toes,
the colors of your skin
and the crevices of your heart.

come love, step out.
we will go round the house we built
with no rooms, shingles or rafters,
but with river boundaries, desert walls
and the alcoves of tree boughs.
i will show you where you began in my mind.
i will tell you the first words you spoke.
i will name the moment of my captivity.

if then you smile and press my hand,
this tale will become told and true.


## JOURNEY

This country of ashphalted roads,
serpentine rows of cut wheat
stubbing through light scattered snow,
must give way
to a sparser ground,
and then to sand
with triple imprints of bird feet,
to a sea rolling and brooding over itself,
to farther catamarans.

And then the palm fronds
that hold aloft the bare blue sky,
crows in argument,

naked children,
mud covered and swift footed,
leaping from rock to rock
as monkeys watch
from atop the roofs
of wayside temples.


## CAPTIVE

anchored,
i dream of other lands:

masses of brown earth floating by,
dense-covered with vegetation,
speared by rivers,
and pierced by raised mountain heads.

i see them drift nearer
to my confinement,
see them erode and displace the sea
that mocks my tethered limbs.

they slip beneath my feet,
gathering me
in a vast expanse of life;
i am no longer captive
but a mere anchorite
choosing his final ground.

# GARDEN: KYOTO (JAPAN)

our journeys end
in a small garden
of pebble and rock;
beatific buddhas
contemplate
sparse blades of grass
fine needles of fir
fathom light
our unshod feet.

this is squirrel time
and small-cloud time:
all things pass
with the slanted sun;
the rock island floats
on a sea of sand,
carrying our minds
to a brimless land.

here life is a mere
state of mind,
sweep of eyes
along the gravel heap,
the trembling of an
upturned leaf.

# Uma Parameswaran

## MEMORY POEMS

### 1. Vigilance

This is where we are now.
We
Who once raised hell on campuses
and stormed citadels of power
and brought dons and deans to their knees;
Who once raised lovers to passionate pitch
till clouds reverberating across continents
thundered down in torrential rain;
Who once raised our nurslings
tending and crooning them to golden wings;
Who once sang from sea to sea,
sweeping rivers into a chorus of joy
and passed each other never touching;
Now
have come together to hold hands,
silenced by missiles from powers that be,
in silent thought for those by lovers slain
or randomly killed by antifeminist rage,
mutely mourning children streetwise but unspared.

We
Who soared into skies of endless desire in our men's arms
Who kissed asleep and hugged awake our children with a
prayer,
now start the day holding each other,
in thought or telephone wires to say,
Take heart, hang in there.

O my sisters, my loves,
as we circle the flame
that once was Wilma, Susan, Anne-Marie,
Michele, Sonia, Genevieve,
do we know, how not know,
it is our own Vigil we hold
in quiet despair.

(March 23–24, 1990)


## 2. *Past Selves*

We have our metaphors,
our favorite pegs on which we hang
our selves.
Life, one says,
is memory and memory
golden grains stored away
from nibbling time.
And then there is K, feeling
her bruised finger's laboured tracing
of her name on her own gravestone
that she stumbled on one day.
And J, her pots of geranium waving
smiling dancing while she in bridal finery
lies on thin ice reaching out for the naked mannequin
floating just below the surface of a fast freezing pool.

Love between friends, one said, is handcrafted—
slender vases inlaid with silver bidri,
filigreed marble from Fatehpur Sikri,
lacquered tables painted on the sands of Thar.

Mine is not anguished or exquisite like theirs
but not quite so crude as it first sounds—
A jigsaw puzzle—fit metaphor for me
who earn my bowl of rice tracing how the pieces
all two thousand of each poem each tale
interlock to form the scene on the box cover

beneath which lie other pictures palimpsest
or parallel mirrors leading us beyond whatever is.

Love between friends. I thought in my plain prairie tongue,
was three thousand interlocking pieces
shaping slowly and forever
the foreground cabin and beds of flowers
azalea phlox hyacinth mid pinecones
against breathtaking purple tints of snow slopes
that meld into the hundred shades of endless sky.

But now I find love between friends
is a six-piece preschool puzzle
to be put together with closed eyes.
A tear
quickfixed for children's sake
trial separation that
after squabbling over custody
and assets
is made final,
the same sordid sequence
as I daily see around me
clogging lawcourt drains.
                    (March 19–23, 1992)


## 3. December 6, 1993

My sisters, my loves,
When
we circled the flame
That once was Susan, Wilma, Anne-Marie,
Michele, Sonia, Genevieve;
When
we came together again and again
with other candles, other names,
but always the same pain,
to hold hands around the flame
that once was sister, lover, child;

When
we cried for women brutally slain,
and grieved we had to come so often
to hold hands around the flame . . .
Oh then
there was so much power around us and within
that I could have reached my arms across the stars
and touched the Mother's face and said,
I am home at last
among my sisters, my loves,
with whom one day I shall meet in joy
as I meet here in pain.

But now,
though the Mother's eyes still smile on me
from intergalactic space,
my sisters move along the halls
on other sides of other walls.

O my sisters, my loves,
can we come together only in grief
and never in joy?


## 4. Memory Is a Thresher

Memory is a thresher, she said,
who flails the husk and stores away
from nibbling Time the golden grain:
happy hopscotch hours
learning of reefknots   slipknots   morsecode,
the newborn's clutch upon your breasts,
the thousandth phallic touch so much richer than the first.

Fool, I said (of late I've had less
and less patience with her)
Self-deluding dolt. Memory is a sieve
that lets the grain fall through and retains the grit.
Only stones remain:

the heavy silence of white-not-blue report cards.
schoolmates whose Kodak smiles lie fading in basement boxes,
sibling deaths that left forever untouched a room of toys.
Only stones remain:
the many miscarried moons of wasted blood,
the many futile probes that could not reach
the pulsing spiritlip that numbed to stone,
the many friends who made their thirty pieces
and never once thought of hanging themselves.

Seal your lips, woman, for Memory
is an old bitch waddling thru the dumpyard
flapping her dozen dry tits
at which pups long dead once drew sustenance.

# Sasenarine Persaud

## THE MAN WHO WENT OVER NIAGARA FALLS IN A BARREL

We avoid the tunnels and those people
who don yellow raincoats (later discarded on benches)
and peer up to the rim.
We have been there too, on observation towers
walled in from the water we should have loved.
It might have been for show. Tourist boots,
tongues vainly   trying to   taste themselves above
the roar.
London cockney, a babble of Paris—or
is it Quebec? Hindi from the U.P. heartland!

The rustling yellow coats were made in China.
On the American side yellow blobs inch along rails.
We watch ice-green water dash around the goat's island
and become white with fright from the fall,
turn the sickly green lube we poured into
two-stroke motorcycle engines of memory—
far away in a tub boat are the other people we avoid
these days. Once we too, curious, donned those
mechanic-blue heavy coats on *The Maid Of The Mist*
to get nearer.

The clever tunnels we avoid: little portholes
in the rock face peering up under the throbbing
white skirt where you nibbled the line from
Steinbeck in an ear. Our boots were soaked.
It was cold but we were in love and you wondered—
After so many trips and so many friends

174

gasping in awe or camouflaged disappointment—
why I never wrote a line.

All these years and excursions did not produce
one memorable word. We have grown older together
and have nobody to show—
nothing.

Along the shore birds chirp. Orange leaves
embrace the green ground, warm fingers
touch red nails in the crowdless dusk
and sitar-silenced souls.

It is good to be away from the noise of the fall
you whispered.

Only today a man went over the edge
unconscious.
He told the press he would not do it again.

In the morning I must tell you
how your sleep energizes
and your breathing makes metre.

For now insomnia.
I remember we avoid tunnels
and noisy yellow raincoats,
dumb nights and numb mornings.

## GIFTING THE LIGHT OF THE SOUL

And I had abandoned them, I knew that there
sitting in the transport, in the sea-quiet dusk . . .
There was nothing they wanted, nothing I could give them
but this thing I have called "The Light of the World"
                    DEREK WALCOTT, "The Light of the World"

They sent me little packages of pepper and thyme,
the condiments of India in tight-lipped bottles
of mustard oil chatney pickle and brine, and once
even a coconut branch broom—but no word no note
which spoke of the land and no letter which would
uncover the hurt. I did not return, I did not return
to the picture in the August grass. K kneeling
and aiming a toy gun at the photographer, somebody
placing a cricketer's cap on my head, another
thumbing sunlight at the camera lens; ma's smile
in the little girl's eyes near the bank of pepper
and thyme. We were once together after ma died
and they walled her in—mamoo coming too late
from the bush on his face. He too returned
to the dredges and the forest like Rama in banwaas,
returned to the diving on the riverbeds for
diamonds and gold: little fragments of self
remaindered in the east; the plane stuck in the
muck of a mountain airstrip, and when finally
the rain lifted and he flew to the coast again
it was too late—pa already fleshless and the pyre
down to ashes. Mamoo finally wrapped the dhoti
and made offerings to the fire, puja to the manes
and puja to the world.

                    It was too late.
I had set out for my soul with memories
of wild birds pecking from the palms
of pa standing in the wind—if the new house had
nothing it must have a verandah touching
the purple starapples closing on the grey

goldenapple branches, freckled with lemon butterflies
and fan-necked lizards wary of the slyeyed sleepy cats.

They stood aside
and let me scatter those ashes of the girdle we
had come from, unburnt pieces of pelvic bones
commingling with red hibiscus, milk-and-purple
madar, mauve jasmine and pink oleander. They
set me out alone on the bow of the boat

in the ocean, let me out alone with the blessing
and the darshan: I the Sanskritist uttering
the ancient prayer to the drumming waves on
wooden guardrail, salt spray on greenheart planks
on cotton on eyes on hands relinquishing the petals
and the ashed bones.

I could not return
and they wept for me. To go and be great and
come back empty hearted. Unreturning progress
reports and their pride in the writing.
All the love, ah the love—but when
the returning—unuttered and unwritten.

They send me little
packages, parcels of pepper and thyme—and the
condiments of India in bottled pickle and brine.
But I could not return and could send them nothing
save the songs of a wandering brahmin
and the fastidious yogi silence.


*mamoo:* maternal uncle.
*banwaas:* forest or exile.
*puja:* worship or prayer ceremony.
*darshan:* vision of the divine, blessing.

## ARTWORK OF KALI

This fleck
this little spittle light dancing
in the dark is all you left me.
It is enough to guide me to the garden.
I would avoid thorns but you loved roses.
This tongue you see me loll is not
for blood. Control of senses, you said
and she is master!
The sculptor mimics
memories of twitching vulva,
red lips firing dark hair curling
to control was all you taught me
left me
this fleck
this little spittle on the lingum tip
this little light dancing through
the drawn blind!

## POSTCARD TO A SISTER IN SOUTH AMERICA

This lilt of light in rain
clouds swarming sun over woods
bleached of leaves except the spruces'
sticking of sky in answer to rusting
oaks remaining willows ripening
like August oranges bowing down
limbs catching blessings of finch
kiskadee blue sakie bunting

This lilt of light in last night's
cotton wicks in oil in diyas
marking Ram's returned to Awadhpuri
with his bride—yes the waiting
for the last jay calls to go south

sparrows chirping chickadees tweeting
the tip of the days of the long nights

To meet again off Karahi-holed roads
clasping the dust from wings of sugar
cane stalks the thousand limbed coconuts
swirling Shiva's dance over browntongued
creeks nipping the ocean your sons celebrate
not this lilt of autumn light; the blooded
childhood sunshine of cannotleavebehind.

# Ian Iqbal Rashid

## AN/OTHER COUNTRY

All this new love of my parents' country:
We have bought the videotapes together,
bought the magazines and books,
all the advertisements,
each others' responses.
We watch the slides of your visit.
Your handsome face tanned, surrounded by mango trees,
planted above the poverty,
the moist beauty,
(which you think of blowing up and then framing,
building into your walls)
majesty imposed upon majesty.

Now I watch you watch Sergeant Merrick watch poor
    Hari Kumar.
And follow as the white man's desire is twisted,
manipulated into a brutal beating.
You are affected by the actor's brown sweating
body supple under punishment. What moves you?
The pain within the geometry of the body bent?
The dignity willed in the motions of refusal?
A private fantasy promised, exploding
within every bead of sweat?
Or is it the knowledge of later:
how my body will become supple
for you, will curve and bow to your wishes
as yours can never quite bend to mine.
What moves you then?

My beauty is branded into the color of my skin,
my strands of hair thick as snakes,
damp with the lushness of all the tropics,
My humble penis cheated by the imperial wealth of yours.
Hari's corporal punishment, mine corporeal:
Yet this is also part of my desire.

## HOT PROPERTY

On the phone with you
trying heroically to save myself and failing
and I hear a click—yet another call waiting.
Inspiration—I decide to pretend
I'm drowning, my dark body
just barely visible in steam rising through a break,
flailing about below a frozen body of water,
helpless, unaccustomed to the cold,
coming from a tropical climate and all.
Save me. You do the work.
But you are annoyed, won't play
you see a different kind of transparency,
no ice, no danger of freezing.

Click quickly to the next caller
and become a mouth piece,
confident oracle if I am believed,
and I am, all the wisdom of the East
messenger, who has never been east of Montreal,
messenger who has not yet been revealed.
Even when I'm mute, it seems,
this one gathers my saliva in buckets
as it drips from my parted lips
and strains for discovery.

I click back
and you're still there

watching me now as I tread water.
The climate's become milder and I'm willing to swim.
You're willing to pull me onto terra firma.
A fair ground.
But in the same moment:
I catch my dark self swimming gracefully
in the mirror frame. Tropical fish.
I see a hook.
New trick.
It's simpler to stay put and wait.
Haul the fisherman in.

# COULD HAVE DANCED ALL NIGHT

I.

I once used to dream of being held knowingly by a man
on whom I would not look.

Then this all came again, the embrace held
in the ease of a dance, held within your hands small
yet capable and roped with thick vein.
And when I tried, it didn't surprise me
to be able to look into your eyes like mine,
the rough color of night, into your shy, pie face.

Standing together tonight I long for the anise
taste of Thai basil on your skin,
your ass and thighs resplendent
in strobes of evening's light.
Tonight I would dance with you across an alien landscape.
We could fly. ("I'm positive.")
But this night finds our legs rooted, knotted,
planted painfully like a flag. ("I've tested positive.")

## II.

Tonight, I watch you walking away,
wheeling your burden before you into the night.
Fists jab my thighs on either side.
Fists which mean to unclench hold
fingers which mean to interlock
with yours, like pieces of a puzzle
join into a picture of two men dancing.

Tonight movement is limited:
from hand to mouth to mind.

Tobacco, caustic laughter in the lungs,
the careful sipping of our herbal teas—
the careful sipping of our everything-will-be-all-rights.

## A REDEFINITION

I lie here on this vast rumpled ocean, your bed,
completely naked but for my skin
which is also a sheath.
This sheath itself you can make a weapon, and a fine one:
It gleams nut brown or bronze or cocoa
or other such magazine words
polished by the sucking of maggots and pests,
waxed, with a veneer of spice and feces,
washed by urine which men have spurted against
makeshift dwellings by which I have lain.
I am a catastrophic beauty (this will make you smile)
—an insistence of immortality.
Through my pores are amplified the shouts
of street merchants and photogenic urchins,
(this makes your smile disappear, yes?),
the offensive cries of burning brides,
hopeless milk screaming inside their searing, succulent,

honey-colored breasts. Listen carefully: hear
the music, melting, bubbling beyond . . .
so sweet, so sweet . . .

I am not even a complication, not worthy
of being one. My words enter the clarity
of your gaze like a blade but what comes back
is cornflower blue, dazed, a trifle
embarrassed, no hurtful words, no afternoon
television dramatics . . . you reach for me, large
white spider against my darkness and I am
yours, now and for the first time.
For you see, my big, blonde, perfume-soaked Sahib,
you have, through your polite—your civilized—grace,
brought down my New World.

# Carol Roh-Spaulding

## DREAMS AT BREAKFAST

I woke as a girl
to my parents' easy
murmur over eggs, rice, and barley tea.
Before the boilers roared
to life in the backroom laundry
or Mother released the leftovers,
snipped napkins in two.
Before the first bus passed
in the street, already exhausted.

In minutes
my father would cross that street
to the barbershop, his fish
and kimch'i in a country tin.
Mother's too floral
bathrobe would shimmer on its
hook til long past nightfall.

But first in the hushed
churning quiet
they told one another
their dreams.
Not the ones you think:
*house of our own, a little*
*put aside, daughters married off*
*citizenship*

but of wings pulsing
at your ear,

someone who had promised
always to be with you
dissolving into the
throng, a longing
thick with the bliss
of your one sure life

And let's not forget flying.

Not like the river would
smoothing itself over all
your surfaces, adorning your hair
with bugs and twigs,
only to lure your ears inward,
make your lungs suck shut. No,
the monks are patient men.
Say you set out
at fourteen, orphaned
hungry. At thirty, ready
to renounce the world.
At sixty-six, seeking
the one thing you never would ask for
in the last place
we thought you would look.
We have a name for this,
same as a river's longing.
Go. Speak it like a password.
As late as it is now,
they could still be waiting.

# HAN

*For Roh Jung-Soon 1895-1992*

This isn't the world we want.
This isn't the world
we hoped for. When
we were only children, spirits
bumbled into your room, glided
across water, stole into your soup.
Tigers tamped the forest floor,
slit-eyed, sated, waiting.
The river Han took down
many a man and woman
in one cold swallow.
These are only some of
the things we knew.
Over the winter village
the Kumgangsan shuddered
blue. Summers, white
shadows beat into
our shit-lined fields.
We grew
and the rice grew.
In the high meadows, monks beat
their drums, stoked their fires
chanted for all of us
in words even they
didn't understand. They
lived on honey wine, sesame cakes,
pine nuts, paulownia blossoms.
If you are ever lost enough, they will
take you in.

## INNER ROOMS

The distance I felt for the country at first passed into an interest
which is almost affection, and on no previous journey have
I made dearer and kinder friends, or those from whom I parted
more regretfully.                    ISABELLA BIRD,1831–1904

Madam Bird plodded down
from the high meadows with one donkey
just for her things.
It was the end of the century, she was travelling light.
Already she had seen more of
my country than I would ever see.
Now she believed in the audacious
tiger, the cold swallow of the Han,
the intense bowl of heat brimming
peaks ancient to her light eyes.
Tong, her Chinese guide, wore
a smile we knew she couldn't read, but spoke
her English passably. From him
we learned that the sole blue shadow,
fresh, aging and erect, was hers.

I was born in the month and year
of the last *Kurdong*, the king's spectacle
along the shit-lined streets of extra-
mural Seoul. South from there
my mother taught me to draw
water, to plant, pluck and hull
rice from which you nip weevils
and silverfish before boiling.
We hung seaweed, candied strips
of persimmon, salted mackerel for
those who passed through our rooms.
If I had been the daughter
of a yangban, I would not have known
what it is to walk in daylight or
watched wine darken the eyes
of travelling students, dignitaries, Japanese.

In no more than a hot, clean
closet, she laid out a steel pallet,
an upended trunk, notebook, lantern.
The oiled paper in the doorway trembled
with the curiosity of onlookers.
Children were excused from sleep. Men had
all the more reason to drink.
After midnight, the muffled silhouette
reclined, and when they knew for certain this
was their only chance, their desperation
buckled and swelled, the paper, shorn of pretense,
carpeted the way as women sniffed,
plucked the hairpins from the soft gray
circled deft palms over fine leather,
evenly woven cotton, clear burning glass.
Eyes glazed like a nursing mother, she waited.

A preacher's daughter, young woman of ill
health, rises at forty, sails to America
scales the Rockies with a buccaneer called Jim.
Marries, not Jim, but now nothing
can stop her. Malaya, Japan, Tibet,
Persia, Manchuria, Kurdistan. What kind of
barbarians allow their women to
roam as though the world were
an untended meadow?—asks a woman-child
with impeccable posture, swaddled
in the richly lit silks of
her inner rooms. But I only wanted
to ask what sort of walls, what ceiling
had housed this woman's uncommon
courage all those years. Later, in a century
she would not come to remember,
I crossed one of her oceans.

Even if we'd had a common
language, what result? She returned
to tell of our good coloring and straight noses,
our play with demons, our willingness to abide

in filth. What rooms had she escaped, having
come all that way not to know us?
Still, when older, I married
a photograph, sailed with a black and white
faith—not in gleaming streets or
handsome features, nor in work, though
I worked, nor vows, which I kept.
Faith of the winged, not quite
fugitive. What you don't know might some day
lift inside you, rise like tide,
nausea, desire. After all your miles of
waiting, that's what soars.

# Gerry Shikatani

## GAS STATION, VOCABLES

even here we do
not escape.
wide asphalt, sheen
of gasoline, moon.
streetcar tracks glaze
silvery for miles, on King Street
high-pitched sound,
buildings closed, alarm-set
wholesale houses for shoes,
import houses / closed.
> (a car's movement
> from behind, turns left
> up ahead / another dark road.

a maple tree, branches caught in
overhead wires the moon's
light
in my throat
breathe this air of tinders,
a flush of exhaust, a moment
of rain, where the yellow lights
of a gas station.

here the sound of clapping
hands move in my hands
even in the angular silence
this city, my home
the vocables delight
/ and darting eyes

spark in shadows,
fill my mouth
with clapping and
the dance of lungs.

## ON AN AFTERNOON

1.
what I hurled was a descent of sparrows
a foraged pocket of words kept gloomy in
the mouth with a single green tooth, it was the plain
truth of newspaper contradiction. "Life is a short patter before
the mongolling of death," a curious traffic of words
across accident-prone city streets, long breaths of literate
                                              exaltation

reducing of being
from tangled thought's
strands feeling, breath
and line a
memory of touch
stone cancel
'd breath
to.

## SPEECH

2.
into the breach of time
and word, habit of speech.
feeling / mouth.

canker sore.
in the mouth.

tongue explores the pain, through
which we see. or tastes divine
of sauteed food and wine stick
in mouth, feeling. this long
measure's reach, a prisoner's
parole. Parole is what we are
what happens at the end of speech.

it's actually falling, like from that
previous line, word.
each passing word, hurls out
the guilt of what time
it is.

## PARKED CARS

3.
I don't care about its ease,
movement of words, making a
play for the Big One. or her, aw,
fuck, shit, aw shit I can't write
anymore, hearing resonance of bumbling
images trapped like pillow
words. no longer knowing the exact
feelings: about love,
about image or right action,
compassion. fuck it. or some other
telescopic.

here, standing. parked cars. parked.
cars. there's no way
around. no way
around
them.

## AS IS

dream and moon incessant rattle
at my door, outside
strong gust and cedar
blows in front of this win-
dow. my brothers, my sisters
who've slid me coins
through years. sometimes a bag
of potato chips sometimes
a bottle of pop. each second
figures walk past
this window elude
hand's clasp. my own brothers
sisters, you all die eventually
just dream and moon left
here. again. cedar blows
in front of this window,
the pauses and words
rattle into place.

## CADAQUES

Cadaques was the sun
and her dream she remembers.
up on the hilly
narrow stone streets
to the old white church.
up through the village
    a swimsuit in a shop.
octopus, squid, anchovies, mussels.
the sea water on her
eyelids
and the night filled
a snail.

Cadaques, Cadaques
the sun, sky of the sea,
blue: and breezes to shore
drinks of carbonated lemon
at bright Catalan cafes, the
    bottles
emptied and Cadaques
of her past.
    the dust was a cloud that
subsided each step
in hot sun. and the huge
pots of red flowers sat
on garden terraces. Mediterranean.
the sea with us, the water
bearing purple sea urchins which
we cut open and ate.
Cadaques was the sun,
    cleared into
the sun.
she sketched on the rocks.

this tiny village, white
on a hillside where
women sold their fish
in the mornings.
                our departure was daylight,
shone back over mountains,
Cadaques, the sun,
shifted, in the bus /the past
filtered evenly,
the train moved an inch.

# Cathy Song

## THE POSSIBILITIES OF INVENTION

My first pair of glasses were pink plastic frosted frames.
I wore them bravely throughout the seventh grade
until I got braces.
Then I switched to metal—small oval granny rims
that clashed with the Mexican silver neck rings
! wound around my neck.
I seemed to need the armour,
a girl with good eyes but poor vision,
I could see what others couldn't:
the treachery of cheerleaders
rallying the masses to their cause,
the popular elections rigged
by petty dictators who demanded
conformity even from the lowliest worm burrowed in books.
*A correctable situation.*
*Nothing terminal.*
The optometrist pronounced
when the big letter E got swallowed
into the white wall of his office
and the optometrist himself,
in a blizzard of light,
loomed like the Abominable Snowman
and I couldn't see my own ten fingers
stretched out in front of me.
Near sighted, I wanted to see far,
beyond the static chatter
cluttering my view.
But distance was destroyed
without the curved aid of glass

ground and measured to guide in
the correct path of light.
A path framed in frosted pink plastic
I was prescribed to follow.
I preferred the whirling blur
of the nearly blind—
was it legal?—
the stunning dizziness I achieved
when I lost the clear evidence of things material
to edges that merged and gave off
dangerous smoke: the possibilities of invention.
Shapes shifted so that the familiar
opened bright holes that let in all the light.
Rivalry between forms diminished.
Clouds revealed their identity
only when I chose to touch them
or reluctantly put on my glasses—
when burnished liquor of fur became wood,
a table and chair;
when a column of chilled air
became glass, a common vase;
when the phenomenon in the mirror
yielded disappointment—
my own stunning unspectacular face.


MIRAGE

Dead are the hours
of a bus winding its two o'clock
progress up the slow curves of a hill
that disintegrates inch by inch
in a daily lack of rainfall,
another year of our withering.
The shingled roofs of houses
repeat themselves in the hands of those
who unfurl the same row of laundered shirts on the line,

evaporating precious moisture into the air,
a maintenance that resists the opulent shower tree
drenching our yard with blossoms.
A pool of petals we enter into another
life of dreaming this one tolerable.
Dead are the hours
that gather leaves in the teeth
of an old man's rake,
passing rust through grass,
a razor's comb through stubble,
as if existence requires constant accounting,
even if it's in the accumulation of dead
twigs like tobacco to chew and savour.
Shake the tree of sleep
so that tomorrow
when a neighbors caged bird sings neurotically
there will be relief,
a brief shimmering mirage of leaves.


## WORK

Work brings out
the sweetest sour heat of a man
a less primitive nose would find offensive,
the waves of mushroom rot
Husband of mine
plants daily in my olfactory glands,
they too working overtime,
ferreting out the dank curve of his armpits
that have moved earth, heaved rocks, split wood, hurled a hammer
paddled through ten foot waves,
delivered squalling babies, hauled away Christmas trees,
sawed off deer antlers, or wedged
a hundred pounds of clay.
Seriously afflicted, I have been known

to bury my face in his empty clothes,
soiled shirts hanging limply on a nail hook,
sweat stains as oil soaked as fossil fuel, fueling
my need to inhale the inimitable essence
of the pull and tug, push and shove of sweet grunting labour,
evidence of a man whose energy works to feed me overtime.

## BLUE ROSES

Blue roses, I want
a body of blue roses
in my death sleep,
the one I did not have in this life—
buoyant blue roses running deep,
brimming swollen like a river of petals,
fragrant boats to keep me afloat.
I long for a body
that will wrap me in the fur of desire—
not this chicken bone dream I choke on
in the gritty waking hours of teeth.
I know what I want.
With the body comes desire
interfering with the mind's release.
Don't try to tempt me with thoughts
of the mind's capacity for expansion,
the mind spinning in space.
You can't convince me
it isn't lonely out there,
orbiting in arctic air.
What could be less free
than this idea of transcendence,
the yearning to merge, to gather light,
join mentally with greater forces in heavenly bliss.
I want my kiss
lower down on the ladder's rung,
kisses swollen with blue fire

feathering my mouth with flames,
thorn of the bluest rose
clenched in my dark bush.


## HOURGLASS

Time tunnels its train of twilight—
that blue branch on the turtle's back
swimming the blue distance of mesas.
And the speed with which we are travelling,
perceived as smoke,
carries us into another frame,
night's series of small windows
discrete as the dining car's cutlery.
At each table a single rose
carries a thorn out of a garden long
gone since this morning a woman
has been left standing shadowless in noon's needle,
collecting beads of sweat in an hourglass,
a river's rosary of turquoise
strands pouring through her hands.
The charitable weeds and rust
heap fenders against windshields
where the broken signals of antennae
like alien cacti
interfere with the crow's ragged spiral
home, habitual,
silent from view,
night's shade pulled
in evening ritual.

# *Krisantha Sri Bhaggiyadatta*

## THE DISAPPEARED KEEP TURNING UP

The disappeared keep turning up
on perfectly happy days
In polite conversations that ask about
so and so
In arguments where the very existence
of the disappeared is disputed
On walls where the graffiti
is overgrown with lichen and movie posters
In passing glimpses
of the hair of upturned brooms
In looking in the mirror alone
and finding no one there
or finding several faces you once knew
The disappeared keep turning up
even in the emptied newspaper columns
In the lighted rooms bereft of shadows
And then you find out that the disappeared
exist within large boundaries of land
which you have never visited
in documents which you have never read
under several shovelfuls of earth
and several annual baptisms of snow

they exist in your very backyard in the chair
you are sitting next to
the food you eat
passed under their noses
and then you find out
their existence was only disappeared

from your two small eyes
the numbers addresses and
dates never made
it into your single books
into your one bedroom
so many walls blanked
in your one small mind


## A LITTLE GIRL CRIES FOR WATER

A little girl cries for water.
he gets down from the stage, his speech.
lifts the child to arms
pours water into her mouth.
the crowd goes wild. people dancing.
kicking up dust. touching the ground
he walks on.

He tells the village:
this polios you fed me
is better than all the meat and fish
I eat in Colombo . . .

In every village, when the gentry
bring him food—he picks it up
goes sit with the beggars
and eats with his hand . . .

He's marched thru Colombo
wearing a tattered sarong . . .

there's no one to
out-populist the president,

sudha says:

buddhism in his mouth.
mass murder in his gut.

## DON'T THINK I DIDN'T SEE YOU

Don't think I didn't see you. Don't think I didn't
know you were there.
Don't think I looked away, because I did indeed look away
Don't think I didn't see your eyes so black and so red
Don't think I didn't want to talk.
To ask you so many questions
I just didn't know what to say. I didn't know where to start . . .
Every word was swallowed way down in my throat
So I tried to eat quickly—such good food, i said—
Everything seemed like I tried not to see you
Seemed like I tried not to know you were there
Tried not to look into your red eyes
and looked instead at your son's, don't they look    those eyes
like his father's I said, and I
Saw you look so tired, and so tough,
and look at me kinda like I was wasting your time
Kinda like: not only do we die,
we have to answer questions from the killers
and help construct their alibis and conscience;
so I didn't want to say anything, everything
I thought of seemed so foolish
everything i tried to say couldn't be said
what else is there to say—my, the food is so nice!—
what else is there to ask. everyone knows what happened
everyone just has that look in their eyes
all the children looking seven going on seventy
I couldn't talk to them, and tried to talk kidstalk
but they just looked at me and it was I
who felt like a child, felt I'd lived on borrowed time
time taken from them, an old man acting like a child
grow up grow up they seemed to cry

nandana says there were bodies burning at the corner
and dayanthi the younger one says, ooooh everywhere
        everywhere
near my school there were so many, says Maithri
and little harsha says killed them and threw them away

and they are all under ten . . .

*before they're ten in america the children see*
*ten thousand murders*
*on television, all those no death deaths*
*and now that bush murdered a hundred thousand in a month*
*and a hundred thousand more children are expected to die*
*the magician swings his golf arm,*
*and the death box switches channels*

## THE DEUTSCHMARK DEVALUES (INDIA)

two of the thinnest brown men carrying bulging suitcases for
this dirigible german—lowering herself onto the boat seat
collapsing into stone. impervious. now ignoring
the two brownest thinnest men who
stand respectfully moving imperceptibly. finally
the older one speaks loud. everyone to hear
culi, culi, he demands but she is statue,
albino rock. teutonic ton truck. berlin brick
finally the younger one sticks
his hand out. the german's fingers reach
in her small change bag, putters in her purse
and produces: one rupee, picked up with two fingers
and then hidden in a fist. extends her arm and
drops it into the cup of his hand. aluminum rupee
dull against his calloused palm, immobile incredulous
palm that swayed under bulging suitcases,
her eyelids draw down dark metalled curtains
on her reddening cheeks. and disappear into
a book (herman hesse's siddhartha)
he looks at his palm. widening. at the rupee coin shrinking.

infinite quiet.

then suddenly the boat engines start
heads turn away to the roar
the younger man stares at the boatman
stares at the coin. metal
living on the etched pinkness of his hand.
not once looking at her his hand closes.
drops down abrupt. as if from an old salute.
he turns towards the old man.
"let's go!"

the boatman's body arches, dips the pole into the water
pushes the boat which does not want to move

eddies, circles, ringlets of water enlarge
touch the edge of the land where
the two men stand
watching

# Suwanda Sugunasiri

## CRY OF THE GREAT BIRD

"Plane carrying the country's most powerful crash in Africa"
—*news item*

1.
Stretched wings aerating the arid land
Moscow to Washington, the Great Bird glides
on to the tarmac, pride in its passengers teeming,
shrinking the world in half.

Huddled within panelled oaks under the eagle eye,
the very best concur, signing out wars
setting on its way pigeons in a beeline.
That was forty-five.

2.
Decorated for its role, wearing the decal
in the music of its humming wings the Great Bird
spirit away the best Ho Chi Minh City to Vatican City
shrinking the world by a half and half again.

Glasses lifted, burning the midnight oil
the best compliment, stare, eat up a thousand pads
but viewing in the table mirror their depleting heads
they dash to the Bird in search of solace.

3.
Offering the load to the heavens in uproar
in homage, vibrrrrating in . . to. . . a trance
in a grand finale of a suicidal act

the Great Bird sheds its wings, dousing
the engine with tears wrenched off the think tank,
hiding in hot shame in a yellow, red blanket,
nosediving its anger in heated explosion
as it kisses the earth, renting
m i l e s  a p a r t  heads and limbs
of the very best that failed!

(1988, Seoul, Korea)

## TO FLY AWAY

Cross-legged
he sits
smiling
hand in lap, under the
        d d d d
     o o o   h h h
   b b b  bodhi  i i i
  bbb     t     i i i
       r
       e
       e
     compassion
radiating
a "Come and see," wearing
the cross    kissing
the Torah singing
the Om    praising
Ahuramazda, my
Perfected *tapis d'orient*
rolls
out, receiving
your feet.

"Toss out
in noble abandon the

cross you
bear, walk
the Perfected Cool,
savouring
the Bodhi
shade
massaging neuron
calming the blue
flow.

"In retreat, shall we
not,
in single abandon
go let go let go
in the wind          ~ ~ ~ ~~~ ( ) ~ ~' ~ --- ..
                  ~~~~ ~' ~~ + '
              ~ ~ ~ ~~~~~~~ * --- ...
              ~  ~~ ~~ ~~  #
                  ~~~~~~~~~~~~~~~~~ ///// .......

the new label
bodhi label

"Eyes unsealed
experience
the Full Awakening
name-
less
birthing
the seven smiles
buried within."

            (1983, Toronto)

# THE KNIGHT AT THE SQUARE

(On a visit to China in 1972, the limousine in which the writer was travelling nearly collided with the only other limousine in the laneless but wide Tien Mien Square.)

See these peasants two-wheeling     their ware
adding their flair even at     the Square!
Army trucks cart along     the Red Army hordes
soldiers in tunic     holding on like toads

My trimmings and curtains     as at a ball
waltzing to my music at our     Tien Mien hall
stepping I vroom,     the armoured Knight
roaring to sixty,     yahoo, what a sight!
the soft touch, silk gloves,     the velvet cover
damned right you're,     the key to power!

The weight is right     the passenger a delight
ministers & queens     in their wealth and might
crossing blue oceans     flying by night
all in my power chariot     sleek and white.

In laneless Tien Mien,     I race, I swerve
where I drive     my sole preserve.
These peasants on wheels,     the baggies on trucks
why do they stare?     Their duty to serve.
Buttoned up in uniform     creased, well pressed
My limo and me,     the Revolution at its best.

You, passenger dear,     under my good care,
the panic in your eye,     triggered from nowhere.
No damned rhyme,     indeed no reason.
Soon, I'm telling you,     it'd be high treason.
This, I remind you,     OUR very own Square.
Chairman Mao's     in the chair!

(1972, Beijing)

## LIGHT IN A HURRICANE

(This poem avoids using finite verb forms, to reflect the
Buddhist notion of action with no actor. The state of mind
in the context of the poem *results* from the process of
meditation itself.)

In green green green
the music waltzing,
now flaring up
in a rock n' roll amber
red,
along the floor
panel of my
AM-FM.

The conductor's baton
hyping the
violin's lust the
anger of cymbals,
the despot of the senses
shooting
its missiles
in-quick-succession
through my
mind.

Mask whisked off,
the recognition—
the pleasure cavern
writ large in green amber
and red,
the cross-legged sage
an intransigent rock
in a bullying
hurricane.

Mind-moments later
green to red in flight
the white monotone

# Arthur Sze

## ORIGINAL MEMORY

1.
White orchids along the window—
she notices something has nibbled the eggplant leaves,

mantises have not yet hatched from the egg.
"*Traduttori, traditori,*" said a multilinguist

discussing the intricacies of Hopi time and space,
but the inadvertent resonance in the mind

is that passion is original memory:
she is at the window pointing to Sagittarius,

she is slicing *porcini* and laying them in a pan,
she is repotting a cereus wearing chalcedony and gold earrings,

she is judging kachinas and selecting the simplest
to the consternation of museum employees.

Grilled shrimp in olive oil—
a red sensation pours into his thought and touch:

the sfumato of her face,
shining black hair reaching down to her waist,

he knows without looking the plum
bruises on her thigh from the spikes of a sectional warp.

2.
The multilinguist wants to reveal the locations
of shrines on the salt trail in the Grand Canyon

but has been declared persona non grata by the tribe.
He may have disproved the thesis that the Hopi language

has no referents to time, but his obsession led
to angers and accusations, betrayals and pentimenti:

a cry of a nuthatch vanishes into aquamarine air.
Some things you have to see by making a pinhole,

holding a white sheet of paper at the proper focal length?
To try to retrace the arc of a passion is to

try to dream in slow motion a bursting into flame?
You are collecting budding yellow tea plants;

I am feeling a sexual splendour in a new orchid leaf.
What is the skin of the mind?

How do you distinguish "truth" from "true perception"?
When is an apex a nadir and a nadir an opening into a first
world?

Italians slice *porcini,* lay them on screens in the sun,
let the maggots wriggle out and drop to the ground.


3.
She is tipping water out of a cloud.
By candlelight, face to face,

the pleasures of existence are caught in a string of pearls.
He remembers her rhythm in a corn dance,

notices the swelling of her left ear from a new earring.
He does not want any distortion—

red leaves falling or beginning to fall,
bright yellow chamisa budding along a dirt road,

snow accumulating on black branches—
to this moment of chiaroscuro in which their lives are a sphere.

Face to face, by candlelight,
the rock work and doorways form a series of triptychs.

She remembers hiking the trail up to Peñasco Blanco,
sees the Chuska Mountains violet in the west,

and, below, the swerve of Chaco Wash,
the canyon opening up: ruins of rock walls

calcined in the heat, and, in red light,
swallows gathering and daubing mud along the cliff face.


## IN YOUR HONOR

In your honor, a man presents a sea bass
tied to a black-lacquered dish by green-spun seaweed.

"Ah" is heard throughout the room:
you are unsure what is about to happen.

You might look through a telescope at the full
bright moon against deep black space,

see from the Bay of Dew to the Sea of Nectar,
but, no, this beauty of naming is a subterfuge.

What are the thoughts of hunters driving
home on a Sunday afternoon empty handed?

Their conception of honor may coincide
with your conception of cruelty? The slant

of light as sun declines is a knife
separating will and act into infinitely thin

and lucid slices. You look at the sea bass's eye,
clear and luminous. The gills appear to move

ever so slightly. The sea bass smells
of dream, but this is no dream. "Ah,

such delicacy" is heard throughout the room,
and the sea bass suddenly flaps. It

bleeds and flaps, bleeds and flaps as
the host slices slice after slice of glistening sashimi.


## THE GREAT WHITE SHARK

For days he has dumped a trail of tuna blood
into the ocean so that a great white shark

might be lured, so that we might touch its fin.
The power of the primitive is parallactic:

in a museum exhibit, a *chacmool* appears as elegant
and sophisticated sculpture, as art, but

witness the priest rip the still beating heart
out of the blue victim's body and place it

pulsing on a *chacmool* and we are ready to vomit.
We think the use of a beryllium gyroscope

marks technological superiority, but the urge
of ideologies then and now makes revenge inexorable.

The urge to skydive, rappel, white-water kayak
is the urge to release, the urge to die.
Diamond and graphite may be allotropic forms
of carbon, but what are the allotropic forms

of ritual and desire? The moon shining on black water,
yellow forsythia blossoming in the April night,

red maple leaves dropping in silence in October:
the seasons are not yet human forms of desire.


## WHITEOUT

You expect to see swirling chunks of ice
flowing south toward open water of the ocean,
but, no, a moment of whiteout as
the swirling ice flows north at sunset.
In a restaurant with an empty screen,
a woman gets up and sings a Chinese song
with "empty orchestra" accompaniment.
Prerecorded music fills the room,
and projection from a laser disc throws
a waterfall and red hibiscus onto the screen.
You are not interested in singing and
following the words as they change color
from yellow to purple across the cueing machine.
Instead, you walk out on blue-green glacier
ice and feel it thin to water in spring.
You notice two moose along the thawing shoreline
browsing for buds, and see the posted sign
"No shooting from here." But "here" is "there."

## ICE FLOE

Nails dropped off a roof onto flagstone;
slow motion shatter of a windowpane;
the hushed sound when a circular saw cutting through plywood
stops, and splinters of wood are drifting in air;
lipstick graffiti on a living room wall;
cold stinging your eardrums;
braking suddenly along a curve, and the car spinning,
holding your breath as the side-view mirror is snapped by a sign pole;
the snap as a purple chalk line marks an angular cut on black Cellutex;
dirt under your nails,
as you dig up green onions with your bare hands;
fibre plaster setting on a wall;
plugging in an iron and noticing the lights dim in the other room;
sound of a pencil drawn along the edge of a trisquare;
discovering your blurred vision is caused by having two
                                        contacts in each eye;
thud as the car slams into a snowbank and hits a fence;
smell of a burnt yam;
the bones of your wrist being crushed;
under a geranium leaf, a mass of spiders
moving slowly on tiny threads up and down and across to
                                        different stems.

# Nguyen Chi Thien

## THEY EXILED ME

They exiled me to the heart of the jungle
Wishing to fertilize the manioc with my remains
I turned into an expert hunter
And came out full of snake wisdom and rhino fierceness.
They sank me in the ocean
Wishing that I would remain in the depths
I became a deep sea diver
And came up covered with scintillating pearls.
They squeezed me into the dirt
Hoping that I would become mire
I turned instead into a miner
And brought up stores of the most precious metal
No diamond or gold, though
The kind to adorn women's baubles
But uranium with which to manufacture the atom bomb.

(1972)

# IN OLDEN DAYS

In olden days Li Bo looked up to the moon
Then looked down thinking of his native land
Nowadays I look up—to find cobwebs
Look down to kill bedbugs and pick up leftover rice
In his inebriation Li Bo could put his feet on the
    Tang emperor's tummy
Famished, my feet rest on rusty chains
Li Bo lived under a Dark Ages monarchy
A tyrannical and feudalistic regime to which freedom
was an alien concept
Me, I live in the age of communist plenty
Of happiness, freedom and this worldly Paradise
Ah unlucky Li Bo and lucky me!

(1967)

# TREE: THE WIND COMES

Tree: the wind comes to caress it
Night: the soft moon is here to brighten it,
    lovingly
Hill: the white clouds hang above its peak
Reeds: the river washes them as it sings them to
    sleep
Sound: the rocky cliff sends back a long echo
Me: a crumpled shadow on the beach!

(1960)

# I MET YOU

I met you within four barbed wire fences
Sunken cheeks and eyes
Tubercular lungs, bloated legs
A cold wind gusted and wailed through the valley
You doubled up and shivered, covering your thin chest
Watching you, even the security doctor had to stop
    his threats
You sit and fit so snugly
In the midst of a chilled, yellow sick huddle
Cough cough
Thick, colored spittle
Your entangled hair falling down
You are a shrunken body, naked. . .
Why the shame when you have nothing left?
You are Misery incarnate
With last night's tears still leaving traces
On your pallid cheekbones
In my heart which has long since grown dark
Tears were on the verge of falling at seeing you.
I took a firm hold of your hand which slightly
    resisted
You looked at me with black, round, innocent eyes
Your pale complexion blushing very slightly.
In your long floating, drifting prison life
It must be a misery to be by yourself, sick!
You must have cried also on many a night
Like last night
Crying for mother and home
For the day you left the beloved South of your
    childhood
The long lost horizon of years ago.
You will realize soon when you are under earth
That your life above it
Has been a burden much heavier than earth itself!
But thinking of the day you will be wrapped in a mat
You must be terrified, I know
When the north wind blows through the pass

Through your flimsy, tattered clothing
And despite your resistance, into your flesh . . .
Do you feel chilly?
Wind and rain everywhere
The valley is waterlogged with mud
The clinic is full of termites, smells mouldy
Pale, sickly, fleshless faces
Look at one another, sustain one another without a
    word
Every few seconds you cough
Blowing your lungs out to pieces
Foaming at the mouth vermilion blood!
You must no doubt hold a big grudge against life
Especially against the Polish ralliers boat*

Which years ago
Swayed on the river
And took you away from the bright, sunny South . . .

Yesterday morning, I held your hand
I wanted to pass onto you a little of my warmth
Despite all the petty prohibitions
this morning you bid farewell to life
Without so much as a whimper
Your corpse is now left on the wuthering hilltop
My soul is a void, torn to shreds . . .

(1965)

* In 1954 the Geneva Agreements divided Vietnam into a Commu-
nist North and a non-Communist South. One million people chose
to go South and 80,000 chose to go North: the latter were called
"ralliers" to the North. Poland supplied the boats that took these
"ralliers" North.

# TODAY MAY 19TH

Today the 19th of May
In bed
I was about to write a poem to cuss Him out
The poetry started to smell like him
When I stopped.
For I thought
A shitty politician like him
Does not deserve
My sweating
To write poetry about
Even though it may be to cuss Him.
Even Marx
His fucking ancestor
Never did get a few lines from me!
So why bother'?
Let the hacks with their prostituted pens
Comb his beard, pat his head, caress his arse!
So I went on to other business
The hell with Him!

(1964)

# Asoka Weerasinghe

## AMATEUR ARCHAEOLOGIST

*For Donald "Haggis" McKenzie*

He left standing the bicycle
propped against a maple tree,
and walked to Becker's where three
pipesmokers clenched their spit-pickled
stems between mesmerized teeth.
Though temptingly unlocked,
no one wanted to ride it,
not wishing to be called a lunatic
or perhaps an eccentric,
with dirt-crusted rubber balls
stuck between wheelspokes;
cracked red celluloid dolls,
rusted rakes, a peeled tin cup
and a torn blanket, all tied up
onto the army-issue bicycle frame
with coir picked along Highway 7.
With a sailor's cap and kilt,
a bizarre form well built
at 60, bicycling at top speed
wanting to be leaf-hidden
among virgin trees, while raking weeds
and soil, of an 1890s kitchen midden,
for archaeological finds of bottlenecks
to festoon his wrinkled, unwashed neck.

# 150 NEWTON ROAD, MUMBLES (1977)

After only a decade
nothing remained of the stone cottage
behind the permanently tilted gate
propped on a rusty hinge,
in Mumbles, Newton Village.
Its ground floor was my refuge
where I read Welsh geology books
in the makeshift study-nook.
In its soot-black coal fireplace
I used to heat at night
an iron witches' pot full of water
to bathe my little daughter.
After only a decade
in Dylan Thomasian Mumbles
nothing remained of this stone cottage
with the creaking stairs
and the Welsh cuckoo clock on the landing
which took me upstairs to the spare
room to sleep. Here the typewriter
on the dresser stood throughout the night
with a blank paper resting on its roller
to thread wards into poems
when I woke up with the morning light.
The climbing trellised rose bush
hugging the stony lichened front wall
I was dejected not to find
erased off the memory of a young mind.
All of this Cymric village beauty
had been gutted and heaped onto a dump,
to make room for a bed of asphalt,
greasy plate glass around a kiosk
and for a Shell Oil petrol pump.

## MEMORIES

Returning to O'Douls
when memories
knocked at the door
of room 204,
I quickly slid the chained
safety lock not wanting
to succumb again
to my haunting
feelings for you.
Walking down Robson Street
the next morning
with my thoughts discreet,
it were your soft lips
that I saw on a mannequin
dressed in a transparent slip.


## ACIREMA FO SETATS DETINU

Yesterday was my present
and today is my past,
I am dead
munching in bed
words like "piss-on-them," a must
with Moore, Stevens and Frost.
With the silencing
of every gunshot
we have wondered why
Hiroshima burnt once
and not five times
during the blast.
And today, Amchitka
knelt in a buddhist samadhi
wanting to touch the sun's
shadow on its grass,
before that blast.

# Rita Wong

## POMEGRANATE DAYS

*:seed one*

sour explode, days in transit
perpetual compromise
not wanting to partake but unable not to

seasonal meanderings
take me in take me out of the uniformed order

brute digestion in fact
economic circumstances in fact

where myth cleaves to fact,
where i might patch together,
where grammar shapes meaning,
where subordinate clauses holler for recognition

spend my days dizzy from bus rides
exhausted fumes on pedestrian streets,

always unfinished,
always movement

*:seed too*

personal ghosts, of which there are too many,
of which i am my own worst

split open papaya,
small pearls spill out,
visceral on fingers, wet signatures:

the woman she could have been,
the woman she is,
negotiation in her very breath,
learning to expand
cool, moist spirit
spirals down her chest
to her pearly toes

lupine and mischievous,
the imp in imperial,
she rivers hungrily to the moon,
flow and ebb, smooth consciousness

miss, missed, missing the boat
so she can swim
in the vessel of herself

*:seed free*

because the red tinfoil is shiny
because the glow is enough
because the traffic light changes and we can move on
forgetting the rules that bound our feet

isolation begets forgetting
collective memory so painful
i want to scratch & scratch my memory
until it bleeds me clean

Rita Wong

*:seed for you*

once bit,
the english apple
must be
chewed & chewed & chewed
jaw tired
and bone weary,
this language has become you
trips up the cantonese stairs

tumble back down,
fall out
from jumping that ocean/
river sticks to skin

home is where your tongue wags
even chinglish sputters
subordinate means under

standard, a yawn
a gap, a flapping jaw,
still chews


*:seed five*

bite your tongue,
memory oozes out.
cause & effect, so clean.

can i swear my mother tongue?
swear it down, swear it blue,
monkeys swear in velvet smooth,
not missing a swing from the boat,
fresh off, i'll chew on compromise
until i learn to like its
tart red taste

*residual seed: sex*

sow                    meet
   sow                              plant
      sow                              print

encode meaning & shudder
littoral stroke

               tentative green
                        tentacle sheen
would growth not be threat but spread
heartleaf root inside me

the chew
the traintrack builders' bones
absent women the addendum
sow: to go back
    to go forward
shuttle till the return fixes inside
abundant blackhaired monkeyheads
reverberate
bone echo
crash ocean against mountain graves
residential misgivings an understatement
hazard an occupation

radical means root
sharp seminal taste on tongue
radical mythology accommodate me!
: gingerskinned sisters holler stories

# A WANDERING DAUGHTER'S GRAMMAR

she congregates with nomads
attentive & occasionally settling,
reconjugates self with each meeting:
i am self
I is personae
i & stolen grammar
hoarded carefully in bare hands & forgotten pockets
*aiya! hai been doh ah!*
good fortune, i'm a tough cookie
will bend & trace those words to follow black, black hair,
the sound between my bare thighs as i walk & sidestep,
mimic & repel the values imposed upon me

remember, timidity begets timidity
speak up, girl!

breast: used in conjunction with chicken, evoking fear. breast: in conjunction with lover, a welling, a swelling, of touch & of shyness

lip: to be used as a verb whenever possible

knuckle: outer layer prone to cracks & dryness, punishment in a harsh climate, the work ethic is never enough

back: in the middle, a spot, a star, her mother said, always at her back, a reflexive verb, used with memory, means support, to talk at

liver: term of endearment, perhaps the inner catalyst for relieving the outer dryness guilt: a way of life, can be slowly unset with optimism

sisterhood: towards including mother if possible

# WHEN I TAKE THE POOL CUE

when i aim for the hard little ball & miss
when math & body meet
but coordination can't make it
when it is dark streetside
small town in Shandong province
when it is so heavy humid
when i know i am on their male space, the pool table
when older men kindly tell me
hold it this way
change your fingers
bend lower, concentrate
when i smile polite thanks & then proceed
to hold the stick my way
when i know i will lose this game, their game,
but i will do it my way
when my chinese from china friend asks
"do they have pool in canada?"
when i grit & nod yes,
tempted to lie, no, that is why i
can't play worth beans
when someone is silently counting the score
& i disregard them
when we are looking for something to do
when i am going to blend in or to shock, without effort
when the night is so guarded & red
when i drop the words i don't want
when i practice deliberate amnesia, survival tactics,
when i implicate myself in imperialism
by ignoring the score

(China,1993)

# BLOOD ORANGE

where you expect familiar orange limbs,
bite into violent purple, congealed red surprise,
reluctant juice.

though we never asked to be,
you make us your blood oranges.

be warned: our sangria circus days
will end.

blade abrupt
and flesh-weary of pinup ardour,
we can ourselves through your eyes,
this is how we have survived
to ripen beyond your lids,
to ferment revolution.

no glossy pedestals for us,
we will not settle for anything less than
salty justice, sharp honesty.

while our sisters rot in sweatshops
we cannot sit in crimson pouts
for your prurient, near-sighted eyes.

our spirits roar louder than your dollar,
& can't be bought at the penny-scratched magazine counter.
you see a catalogue of wives for sale,
we see each others' tears.

you don't even understand—
this is not about blood oranges in every supermarket
but the return of forests and rambling wild gardens
of nightwarm women yelling for our lives,
tongues waging wars,
faster than the flash of your rusty silver knives.

# Jim Wong-Chu

## MOTHER

she always wears her silence
in front of father

funny tho

none of us
brothers or sisters
ever woke
when they made love
and that must have been often
because there are many of us
and some knew they were not wanted

those were the days
before birth control pills
and condoms
at least the cheap ones

we were poor

funny tho

father never gave her money
to buy food
preferring to buy it himself
but she fed us
I never understood this

in the morning
she'd be up before us
firing our breakfast *jook*
and after packing us off to school
she'd start her wash
by hand
cold soap water
wooden wash board
hand wrung
headless forms hung on bamboo poles
skewered shirtsleevcs like flags
rows of crucifixes
baking in the dry wind

the day is long
with many goodbyes and hellos
before the night

while we sleep
in our one room home

she mends the last of tomorrow's shirts
and quietly waits

for father

*jook*: congee, rice porridge

# PEASANTS

my father came
from the rice fields
to the city
and there he stayed

just yesterday
I sat and wondered
about all this

what does it mean

rice fields
a glittering city
I try to touch

both ends
are perhaps
a bridge
a causeway
linking rainbows
sunny wet afternoons

from green rice fields
to glittering city
the green and glitter merge

steadily quietly

outside my window
it is raining

today the rain

nourishes rice fields
nourishes the city
nourish me

# FOURTH UNCLE

we met in victoria

we talked and discovered
our similar origins

you a village relative
while I a young boy
sitting quietly on the other side
of the coffee table
cups between us
we are together
for the moment
but 1 feel far from you

you said
you travelled and worked
up and down this land
and now you have returned
to die

to be buried
beside the others
in the old chinese cemetery
by the harbour
facing the open sea
facing home

at the end of my life
will I too have walked a full circle

and arrive like you
an old elephant
to his grave?

# INSPECTION OF A HOUSE PAID IN FULL

I could not hide
my curiosity at your pride
in paying cash in full

perhaps it was
because you arrived
in canada
young and penniless

while working at our restaurant
you came up with the strangest notion
that some day
when you own your own place
you could get away
with substituting ink
for coffee

(cheap profitable imitation)
those wild hopeful impossibilities
made yours a rocky one-man road
up the golden mountain

yet you made it

and today
looking me squarely in the eye
you tell me you have arrived
your family at your side

my last words
are

BEWARE THE TAXMAN

# OLD CHINESE CEMETERY KAMLOOPS JULY 1977

like a child lost
wandering about
touching feeling
tattered grounds
touching seeing
wooden boards

etched in ink
etched in weather
etched in fading memories
etched
faded
forgotten

I walk
on earth
above the bones
of a multitude
of golden mountain men
searching for scraps
of memory

like a child unloved
his face pressed hard
against the wet window

peering in
for a desperate moment
I touch my past

# THE SOUTH CHINA HOMECOMING OF KLONDIKE LEE

you hold your firstborn
for the first time

he sniffles
his blotchy red buddha nose
his tiny face blown like a balloon

the proud grandmother says
he looks just like you

you laugh

your laughter greets the quiet eyes
of your wife

she coughs

making you tuck the folds
of warm blankets closer around her neck

soon they will all be faded images
on a photograph

drawn in solitude

until the edges break
and fall
like snow flakes
onto the frozen caribou tundra

it is winter in your village
and for the first time in ten years
you will miss snow

# About the Contributors

MEENA ALEXANDER was born in India and has lived in New York City since 1980. She teaches at Hunter College (CUNY) and in the Writing Program at Columbia University. Her small magazine and anthology credits include *Daedalus, Grand Street, The New York Times Magazine Review, Making Waves, Writing by Asian Women* (1989), and *Charlie Chan Is Dead: Contemporary Asian American Fiction* (1993). Among her published books are *House of a Thousand Doors* (poetry; Three Continents Press, 1988), *The Storm, A Poem in Five Parts* (poetry; Red Dust, 1989), *Nampally Road* (novel; Mercury House, 1991), *River and Bridge* (poetry; TSAR, 1996), and *The Shock of Arrival* (prose; South End Press, 1996).

AGHA SHAHID ALI, originally from Kashmir, is now on the MFA Creative Writing faculty at the University of Massachusetts, Amherst. He is the author of seven collections of poetry, including *The Half-Inch Himalayas* (Wesleyan University Press), *A Nostalgist's Map of America* (Norton), and the forthcoming *The Country Without a Post Office* (Norton). He is also translator of *The Rebel's Silhouette: Selected Poems* (University of Massachusetts Press) by the Urdu poet Faiz Ahmed Faiz.

HIMANI BANNERJI was born in India and currently teaches sociology at York University (Toronto). A feminist author, she works in the areas of Marxism and antiracism. *The Writing on the Wall* (TSAR) and *Thinking Through: Essays on Feminism, Marxism and Anti-Racism* (Sister Vision) are her two books of essays on culture and feminist theory She has also coauthored anthologies on issues pertaining to gender, race, and class. Her other selected titles are *A Separate Sky* (poetry), *Doing Time* (poetry), and *Coloured Pictures* (children's fiction).

MEI-MEI BERSSENBRUGGE was born in Beijing, China, and grew up in Massachusetts. She is a graduate of Reed College and Columbia University, where she received her MFA. Her work has appeared in many anthologies and periodicals, and she is the recipient of many awards, including National Endowment of the Arts (NEA) grants and the Before Columbus American Book Award. Her books of poetry include *The Heat Bird* (Burning Deck Press), *Empathy* (Station Hill Press), and *The Unbreakable Heart* (Kelsey Street Press). She lives in New Mexico with artist Richard Tuttle and daughter.

SADHU BINNING's books include two volumes of poetry and two of short stories in Punjabi, and a bilingual English-Punjabi volume of poetry *No More Watno Dur* (TSAR, 1995). He edited the literary monthly *Watno Dur* from 1977 to 1982 and coedited *Watan* from 1989 to 1995. He is a founding member of the *Vancouver Sath* and *Ankur* collectives based in Vancouver and has coauthored and produced several plays about the South Asian community. A Vancouver resident (with wife and two children), he works as teacher and a translator. Binning immigrated to Canada from India in 1967.

MARILYN CHIN is on the faculty of the MFA Program at San Diego State University. Her recent poetry appearances are in *The Iowa Review, The Kenyon Review, Parnasus,* and *Ploughshares.* Her awards include the Stegner Fellowship, the Mary Robert Rinehart Award, and NEA awards. She has held residences at Yaddo, the McDowell Colony, Centrum, and the Virginia Center for Creative Arts. She received an MFA from the Iowa Writers Workshop in 1981. Her books of poetry include *Dwarf Bamboo,* and the recent *The Phoenix Gone, The Terrace Empty* (Milkweed Editions, 1994). Born in Hong Kong, she now lives in San Francisco, but San Diego is "her most recent exile."

MADELINE COOPSAMMY was born in Trinidad, studied in India (Delhi University), and has lived in Manitoba since 1969. A certified teacher, she holds degrees from the University of Manitoba and is active in equality rights, especially those relating to immigrant women and education. Her poetry, fiction, and short essays have appeared in many anthologies and small magazines, including *A Shapely Fire: Changing the Literary Landscape* (Mosaic Press, 1987) and *New Worlds of Literatures, Writings from America's Many Cultures* (Norton, 1994).

RIENZI CRUSZ was born in Sri Lanka and came to Canada in 1965. A former Reference Librarian at the University of Waterloo, in Ontario, where he still lives, his poetry has appeared in many small magazines in Canada and abroad, such as *Prism International, Malahat Review, Canadian Forum, Quarry, West Coast Review, Ariel, The Toronto Review* and *Kunapipi.* Among his books are: *Elephants and Ice* (Porcupine's Quill, 1980), *A Time for Loving* (TSAR, 1986), *Still Close to the Raven* (TSAR, 1985), *The Rain Doesn't Know Me Any More* (TSAR, 1989), and *Beatitudes of Ice* (TSAR, 1995). His *Selected Poems* are due for publication in 1997.

CYRIL DABYDEEN was born in South America (Guyana) and has been living in Canada since 1970. Travelled widely across Canada as an activist in antiracism issues, he has taught English for many years at Algonquin College, and Creative Writing at the University of Ottawa. He has published poetry, short stories and essays in numerous small magazines in Canada, the US, the UK and Europe. His poetry books include *Coastland: New and Selected Poems* (Mosaic Press, 1989), *Stoning the Wind* (TSAR, 1994), and *Discussing Columbus* (Peepal Tree, UK, 1996). Among his fiction titles are *Dark Swirl* (Peepal Tree, 1989), *Jogging in Havana* (Mosaic Press, 1994), and *Black Jesus and other Stories* (TSAR, 1996). He was the official Poet Laureate of Ottawa from 1984-87 and lives in Canada's capital.

CHITRA BANERJEE DIVAKARUNI was born in India and received a PhD in English from the University of California at Berkeley. Teaching creative writing at Foothill College, San Francisco, she is also active in South Asian women's issues relating to domestic violence and other abuses. Her work has appeared in periodicals such as *Ms, Good Housekeeping, Chicago Review, Indiana Review,* and *Calyx.* Her writing awards include an Allen Ginsburg poetry prize, a Pushcart Prize, and PEN Syndicated Fiction Project Awards. Among her poetry titles are *Dark Like the River, The Reason for Nasturtiums,* and *Black Candle.* Her recent fiction, *Arranged Marriage,* appeared with Anchor/Doubleday in 1995.

RAMABAI ESPINET teaches at Seneca College and York University, Toronto. She was born in Trinidad, where she completed her academic work. She specializes in postcolonial literature and her published works include *Nuclear Seasons* (1991), *Creation Fire: A CAFRA Anthology of Caribbean Women's Poetry* (1990), and two children's books. Her performance piece, *Indian Robber Talk,* has been staged in Toronto. She is involved in Indo-Caribbean women's issues, both as an educator and community activist.

LAKSHMI GILL came to Canada from the Philippines in 1964 to do an MA at the University of British Columbia. Since then she has lived in many parts of Canada. One of the earliest of the published Asian Canadian writers, her poetry books include *During Rain, I Plant Chrysanthemums* (1966), *Mind Walls* (1970), *First Clearing* (1972), and *Novena to St Jude Thaddeus* (1979). She has also published a novel, *The Third Infinitive* (TSAR, 1993). She currently lives and teaches in Vancouver.

KIMIKO HAHN was born just outside of New York City to a Japanese-American mother and German-American father. Her influences emerge from her Asian background, American poetry, rock n' roll, feminism and cultural politics (she has organized Asian American writers' panels for the American Writers Congress). Her poetry collections include *Air Pocket* (1989), *Earshot* (1992), both from Hanging Loose Press, and *The Unbearable Heart* (Kaya Press, 1995). She has received fellowships from the NEA and the New York Foundation for the Arts and is currently Assistant Professor of English at Queen's College (CUNY). She lives in Brooklyn with her husband and two daughters.

GARRETT HONGO was born in Hawaii, grew up in Gardena, California, and was educated at Pomona College, the University of Michigan, and the University of California at Irvine where he earned his MFA in English. His poetry has appeared widely in magazines such as *The New Yorker, Antaeus,* and *The Nation*; and he has received a number of fellowships, including the Thomas J Watson Fellowship, the Hopwood Prize, and NEA Fellowships. He has taught in Washington and California and currently teaches at the University of Oregon's Creative Writing Program. Among his books are *Yellow Light* (Wesleyan University Press, 1982) and *The River of Light* (Knopf, 1988).

KEVIN IRIE has published widely in many Canadian and other periodicals and anthologies. His books include *Burning the Dead* (Wolsak & Wynn, 1992), and *The Colour of Eden* (Owl's Head Press, 1996), from both of which the poems included in this collection are taken. A Japanese-Canadian (*Nisei*), he is a school teacher who lives in Toronto.

SALLY ITO was born in Alberta and grew up in the Northwest Territories and in Edmonton, where she now is an instructor in English and Creative Writing at the Kings University College. She is a poet and a translator, and her work has appeared in magazines and anthologies such as *Matrix, The Capilano Review, Grain, Dandelion, Poets 88* (Quarry Press), and *Breathing Fire* (Harbour Press, 1995). Her first published book, *Frogs in the Rain Barrel,* came out from Nightwood editions in 1995.

MAY SEUNG JEW has been active in the Asian-Canadian Writers' Workshop in Toronto and in local community work for a number of years.

SURJEET KALSEY was born in Punjab (India) and came to Canada in 1974. She received an MFA in Creative Writing from the University of British Columbia and lives in the Vancouver area. Besides poetry, she writes fiction, and is also interested in "creating therapeutic drama by developing script and directing with totally new people. . . who have been living drama in their day-to-day life." Her books, published by Third Eye Publications, Ontario, include *Speaking to the Winds* (1982) and *Footprints of Silence* (1988).

JOY KOGAWA was born in Canada of Japanese-Canadian parents. She has lived in many cities in Canada and is now resident in Vancouver. The Japanese-Canadian internment during the Second World War has influenced much of her work, reflected particularly in her award-winning novel *Obasan* (Lester & Orpen Dennys, 1981). She began her career as a poet, and her many poetry books include: *A Choice of Dreams* (McClelland and Stewart, 1974), *Jericho Road* (McClelland and Stewart, 1977), and *Woman in the Wood* (Mosaic Press, 1985). She has also written children's books. Her latest novel is *When the Rain Ascends* (Knopf, 1996).

MINA KUMAR is a transportation planner in New York City. Her poems have appeared in *Fireweed, Room of One's Own, Manushi, Wasafiri, The Toronto Review,* and the *Kenyon Review,* and in several anthologies. She has recently published her first book of poems, *Hole* (Hanging Loose Press; and the Women's Press ,Toronto). She was born in Madras, India.

CAROLYN LEI-LANILAU's poetry, essays, and translations have appeared widely in such publications as *The American Poetry Review, The American Voice, Manoa, Amerasia Journal, Chicago Review, The Bloomsbury Review, Yellow Silk,* and *Before Columbus Review.* Her published books include *Wode Shuofa* (My Way of Speaking) published by Tooth of Time, 1988. She was born in Hawaii and now makes her home in Oakland, California.

WING TEK LUM's first collection of poems, *Expounding the Doubtful Points,* was published by Bamboo Ridge Press, 1987. He currently lives in Hawaii.

BHARGAVI MANDAVA is a graduate of New York University; her journalism and literary work have appeared in *The Village Voice, The Bloomsbury*

*Review, Buffalo Spree Magazine, CrazyQuilt Quarterly,* and *The Rockford Review.* Her awards include the Rudin Scholarship and the Joyce Kilmer Prize. Her first novel, *Where the Oceans Meet,* has recently appeared with Seal Press, Seattle. Of Indian origin, she makes her home Los Angeles, California.

DAVID MURA is a *Sansei* Japanese-American who was educated at Vermont College (MFA in Creative Writing). Later he taught at the universities of Minnesota and Oregon, among other places. Straddling genres of poetry, nonfiction, drama and criticism, his books include *Turning Japanese: Memoirs of a Sansei* (Anchor Doubleday, 1996), *The Colors of Desire* (Anchor, 1995), *After We Lost Our Way* (Dutton, 1989), *A Male Grief: Notes of Pornography and Addiction* (Milkweed Editions), and *Where the Body Meets Memory: An Odyssey of Race, Sexuality and Identity* (Anchor/Doubleday, 1996). His small magazine and anthology credits are numerous, including *The Language of Life* (edited by Bill Moyers), *The New American Poets of the '90's, The New Republic,* and *The Nation.* A recipient of many fellowships and residences, he is now Artistic Director of the Asian American Renaissance in Minnesota, where he lives with his wife and three children.

SUNITI NAMJOSHI was born in Bombay, India. After serving in civil service and academic posts in India, from 1972 until recently she taught in the Department of English at the University of Toronto. She has published numerous poems, fables, and articles in anthologies and journals in India, Canada, the US, Australia and Britain. Her books include *Feminist Fables* (Fiddlehead Poetry Books), *The Authentic Lie* (Fiddlehead Poetry Books), *The Bedside Book of Nightmares* (Goose Lane Editions) and, more recently, *Saint Suniti and the Dragon* (Spiniflex Press). She currently lives in the UK.

MICHAEL ONDAATJE was born in Sri Lanka, which he left at the age of eleven to attend school in England. He came to Canada in 1962 and was educated in Canadian universities, notably Queen's University. He teaches at York University, Toronto. His books include *In the Skin of a Lion, Coming Through Slaughter, Running in the Family, There's a Trick with a Knife I Am Learning To Do* , and the Booker Prize-winning novel, *The English Patient.* He is a twice winner of the Governor General's Award for Literature. His films include *Sons of Captain Poetry* and *The Clinton Special.*

S PADMANAB was born in India and currently lives in Saskatoon, Saskatchewan, where he has been active in the local writing community for many years. A medical doctor by training and practice, he is also a painter: he has his "own little gallery" and sells over 50 paintings a year. He has appeared in many small magazines and anthologies in Canada, the US and India. His books include *A Separate Life* (Writers Workshop, Calcutta).

UMA PARAMESWARAN was born in Madras, India, and came to Canada in 1966. She is currently an English professor at the University of Winnipeg; her academic specializations include the Romantics, women's literature and postcolonial literatures. She has served as chair of various professional organizations, such as the Canadian Association for Commonwealth Language and Literature Studies and the Manitoba Writers' Guild. In Winnipeg she organizes a weekly TV show; her published works include *Trishanku* (TSAR,1988), *Rootless but Green are the Boulevard Trees* (TSAR,1988), and *The Door I Shut Behind Me* (Affiliated East-West Press, 1990).

SASENARINE PERSAUD was born in Guyana and lives in Toronto. His work includes both fiction and poetry and has appeared in *Concert of Voices: An Anthology of World Writing in English* (Broadview Press, 1995) and *The Heinemann Book of Caribbean Verse* (1992); among his published books are *Under the Golden Apple Tree* (1996) and *A Surf of Sparrows' Songs* (TSAR, 1996).

IAN IQBAL RASHID was born in Dar es Salaam, Tanzania and has lived in Toronto since childhood. He is also an editor, filmscript writer, and cultural organizer and frequently travels between Canada and the UK. He has published two books of poetry: *Black Markets White Boyfriends* (TSAR, 1991) and *The Heat Yesterday* (Coach House Press, 1996; TSAR, 1997).

CAROL ROH-SPAULDING received her PhD in English from the University of Iowa in 1996 and is now an Assistant Professor of English and Creative Writing at Drake University. Of mixed Korean and Anglo heritage, she is particularly interested in representations and literary expressions of mixed-race consciousness. She has published poems and stories in *Ploughshares, Pushcart Annual XVI, Beloit Fiction Journal, Korean Culture,* and *Amerasia;* her stories have also been anthologized in several collections.

GERRY SHIKATANI was born in Toronto, after his parents evacuated from the tiny northern British Columbia fishing village of Port Essington; he grew up in Toronto's inner city and attended the University of Toronto. He has been active in the Toronto poetry scene since 1973, appearing in many small magazines. Among his books are *A Sparrow's Food* (Coach House Press) and *Poems 1973-78;* he has also edited, with David Aylward, the collection *Paper Doors: An Anthology of Japanese Canadian Poetry* (Coach House Press, 1981).

CATHY SONG was born in Honolulu. She was educated at Wellesley College and Boston University, and her first book, *Picture Bride* (Yale University Press, 1983), won a Yale Younger Poets Award in 1982. Her other titles include *Frameless Windows, Squares of Light* (Norton, 1988), and *School Figures,* University of Pittsburg Press, 1994). She currently lives in Honolulu, Hawaii.

KRISANTHA SRI BHAGGIYADATTA was born in Sri Lanka and currently lives in Toronto. Active in community work, including trade union involvement, he has been writing for the past twenty years, with appearances in many small magazines such as the *Toronto Review* and the *Asianadian.* His poetry books are *Domestic Bliss* (1982), *The Only Minority Is the Bourgeoisie* (1985), and the *52nd State of Amnesia* (TSAR, 1994) from which the poems included here are taken.

SUWANDA SUGUNASIRI was born in Sri Lanka and was educated there and in the US on a Fulbright Scholarship. He is a leader in the Buddhist community in Canada and teaches Education at the University of Toronto. He has edited *The Whistling Thorn: Fiction by South Asian Canadian Writers* (Mosaic Press, 1995) and has published one book of poetry, *The Faces of Galle Face Green* (TSAR, 1995). In the 1980s he directed an important survey and study on South Asian Canadian writing. He is a freelance correspondent for the *Toronto Star* and writes on issues such as multiculturalism and religion.

ARTHUR SZE was born in New York City and attended the University of California at Berkeley. He is the author of five books of poetry: *Archipelago* (Copper Canyon Press, 1995), *River River* (Lost Roads, 1987), *Dazzled* (Floating Island, 1982), *Two Ravens* (Tooth of Time, 1984), and *The Wind and the Willow* (Tooth of Time, 1981). His small magazine and anthology credits are numerous, including *The American Poetry Review, Manoa, The Bloomsbury Review, Harvard Magazine, The Seattle Review,* and *The Open Boat.* His residences, fellowships and awards include NEA grants, the Lannan Literary Award, and the Eisner Prize (University of California at Berkeley). He lives in Santa Fe, New Mexico, and is Director of the Creative Writing Program at the Institute of American Indian Arts.

NGUYEN CHI THIEN was born in 1939 in Hanoi and educated in French and Vietnamese. He spent a total of 27 years in jail for dissident activity in Vietnam. In 1979 a handwritten copy of his collection was passed on to the British Embassy, which brought it out to the Vietnamese diaspora. *Flowers from Hell* resulted, from which some of the poems published here are taken. His first public appearance in the US occurred in 1995; he now lives in Virginia and recently addressed the Joint American Committee of the House of Representatives and Congress. The translation of his poems here is by Nguyen Ngoc Bich, who also translated (with W S Merwin and Byron Raffel) *A Thousand Years of Vietnamese Poetry* (Knopf, 1975).

ASOKA WEERASINGHE was born in Sri Lanka and educated at the Universities of London and Wales, and in Canada at Memorial University as a paleontologist. He has won the Welsh University Eisteddford Poetry Award, the Newfoundland and Labrador's Arts and Letters Gold Medal for Poetry, and the Sri Lanka State Literary Award (1995). His books include *Spring Quartet* (Breakthru, UK), *Kitsalano Beach Songs* (Commoner's Publishing), and *Tears for My Roots* (Today's Men Publications). He lives in Gloucester, Ontario, where he is active on the local poetry scene.

RITA WONG has been associated with the Asian Canadian Writers Workshop and is an editor of *absinthe magazine.* Her work has appeared in *Fireweed, Contemporary Verse II, West Coast Line,* and in the anthologies *Kitchen Talk and The Other Woman: Women of Colour in Canadian Literature.* She has degrees from the Universities of Calgary (BA) and Alberta (MA), and recently received an MA in Archival Studies from the University of British Columbia.

She currently lives in Calgary.

JIM WONG-CHU was born in Hong Kong and brought to Canada as a "paper son." He was raised in British Columbia and has worked in many jobs, as dishwasher and potato peeler, waiter, short-order cook and delivery boy. Educated at the Vancouver Art School, he became an original member of the Asian Canadian Writers Workshop. He is currently a full time letter carrier with Canada Post. His poetry has appeared in such magazines as *West Coast Review, Asianadian, Mainstream, Potlach,* and *Inalienable Rice, A Chinese and Japanese Canadian Anthology,* which apeared in 1979. His has published one book of poetry, *Chinatown Ghosts* (Pulp Press, 1986), from which the poems included here are taken.

# Acknowledgements

Grateful acknowledgement is made to the authors, and in some cases to the publishers for granting permission to reprint the poems, many of which have appeared in previous collections and in literary magazines.

MEENA ALEXANDER: "Relocation," "News of the World," "Brown Skin, What Mask?", "Passion," "Elephants in Heat."

AGHA SHAHID ALI: "The Dacca Gauzes," "A Dream of Glass Bangles," "Snowmen," from *The Half-Inch Himalayas* (Wesleyan University Press); "I see Kashmir from New Delhi at Midnight" from *The Country Without a Post Office* (Norton).

HIMANI BANNERJI: "End Notes," "Voyage," "In This Fugitive Time."

MEI-MEI BERSSENBRUGGE: "Chinese Space," "The Blue Taj," "Tan Tien," "Texas," from *Empathy* (Station Hill Press).

SADHU BINNING: "A Tale," "River Relations," "That Woman," "Parents," "Rebellious Sita," from *No More Watno Dur* (TSAR).

MARILYN CHIN: permission granted by Milkweed Editions for "Tienanmen, the Aftermath," "Beijing Spring," "Elegy for Chloe Nguyen," "Gruel," "Turtle Soup," from *The Phoenix Gone, The Terrace Empty.*

MADELINE COOPSAMMY: "First Hot Dog," "Naomi: Lost Woman," "Roots," "The Second Migration."

RIENZI CRUSZ: "Conversations with God About My Present Whereabouts," "When Adam First Touched God," from *Singing Against the Wind* (Porcupine's Quill); "Elegy for the Sun-Man's Father," from *Elephant and Ice* (Porcupine's Quill); "The Rain Doesn't Know Me Any More" from *Still Close to the Raven* (TSAR) and "After the Snowfall," from *Beatitudes of Ice* (TSAR).

CYRIL DABYDEEN: "For Columbus" from *Coastland: New And Selected Poems* (Mosaic Press); "Declaration," "Horses in the Dark," "My Mother," "My Sundry Life."

CHITRA BANERJEE DIVAKARUNI: "Making Samosas," "Indigo," "The Brides Come to Yuba City," "I, Manju," "The Makers of Chili Paste."

RAMABAI ESPINET: "Hosay Night," "In the Month of the Sturgeon Moon," "Marronage," "Liz," from *Nuclear Seasons* (Sister Vision).

LAKSHMI GILL: "The Man with a Mission," "Time Expired," "Just This," "I Turn."

KIMIKO HAHN: "The Crab," "The Fan," "A Circle of Lanterns," "The Unbearable Heart" from *The Unbearable Heart* (Kaya Press); "Instead of Speech."

GARRETT HONGO: "Ministry: Homage to Kilauea," from *Poetry Ireland.*

KEVIN IRIE: "An Immigrant's Son Visits," "Flight: An Immigrant's Memory," "The Camps: Burning the Dead" from *Burning the Dead* (Wolsak &

Wynn); "Hearts" from *The Colour of Eden* (Owl's Head Press).

SALLY ITO: "Chanson," "Haecceitas," "Seahorse," "The Poor."

MAY SEUNG JEW: "Woman in the Room," "Snow," "When I Get," "Love Song from a Young Lady to an Older Gentleman" from *Asianadian*.

SURJEET KALSEY: "Voices of the Dead," "Against the Wave," "An Eclipse," "Missing Basis" from *Footprints of Silence* (Third Eye).

JOY KOGAWA: "For a Blank Notebook," "She Has Been Here for Three Months," Station of Angels," "Minerals from Stone," "Road Building by Pick Axe" from *Woman in the Wood* (Mosaic Press).

MINA KUMAR: "Mira Awaits Krishna in Riverside Park," "Sandhana," "The House was Dank and Deep," "Leaving."

CAROLYN LEI-LANILAU: "On the Death of Gu Cheng," "Parable," "Hangzhou Never So Good in Oakland," "The Structure of Bill Blake Within Me," "Harry's China."

WING TEK LUM: "On M Butterfly," "An Image of the Good Times," "The Devout Christian."

BHARGAVI MANDAVA: "Hearing Tongues," "Indian Fever," "Absence," "Moonsweets," "Desert Haiku."

DAVID MURA: "The Young Asian Women" from *The APA Journal*; "The Words on my Tongue," "Father Blues for Jon Jong," "Caliban's Curse," "In America."

SUNITI NAMJOSHI: "Graven Images," "Minimal Murder," from *The Toronto South Asian Review*; "Biped," "The Creature," "The Fur Seals as Shown on Television," from *The Bedside Book Of Nightmares* (Goose Lane).

MICHAEL ONDAATJE: "Uswetakeiyawa," "Sweet Like a Crow," "The Hour of Cowdust," "Light" from *There's A Trick with a Knife I'm Learning to Do: Poems 1963-1978* (McClelland & Stewart).

S PADMANAB: "Camel by the Percolator," "Journey," from *Whetstone*; "Captive" and "Garden: Kyoto (Japan)," from *The Toronto South Asian Review*.

UMA PARAMESWARAN: *Memory Poems:* "Vigilance," "Past Selves," "December 6, 1993," "Memory is a Thresher."

SASENARINE PERSAUD: "The Man Who Went Over Niagara Falls In a Barrel," from *The Toronto Review*; "Gifting the Light of the Soul," from *Grain*; "Artwork of Kali," from *Wasafiri*; "Postcard to a Sister in South America."

IAN IQBAL RASHID: "An/other Country," "Hot Property," "Could Have Danced All Night," "A Redefinition" from *Black Markets White Boyfriends*(TSAR).

CAROL ROH-SPAULDING: "Dreams at Breakfast," "Han," "Inner Rooms."

GERRY SHIKATANI: "Gas Station, Vocables," "On An Afternoon (1)," "Speech (2)," "Parked Cars (3)," "As Is," from *Waves*; "Cadaques."

CATHY SONG: "Possibilities of Invention," "Mirage," "Work," "Blue Roses," "Hourglass."

KRISANTHA SRI BHAGGIYADATTA: "The Disappeared Keep Turning Up," "A Little Girl Cries for Water," "Don't Think I didn't See You," "The Deutschmark Devalues (India)," from *The 52nd State of Amnesia*.

SUWANDA SUGUNASIRI: "Cry of the Great Bird," "To Fly Away,""The Knight at the Square," "Light in a Hurricane" from *The Faces of Galle Face Green* (TSAR).

ARTHUR SZE: "Original Memory," "In Your Honour," "The Great White Shark," "Ice Floe" from *Archipelago* (Copper Canyon Press).

NGUYEN CHI THIEN: "They Exiled Me," "In Olden Days," "I Met You," "Today May 19th," from *Flowers From Hell;* "Tree: The Wind Comes."

ASOKA WEERASINGHE: "Amateur Archaeologist" and "Acirema Fo Setats Detinu" from *The Toronto South Asian Review;* "150 Newton Road, Mumbles (1977)," "Memories."

RITA WONG: "Pomegranate Days," from *absinthe;* "a wandering daughter's grammar," "when i take the pool cue," "blood orange".

JIM WONG-CHU: "mother," "peasants," "fourth uncle," "inspection of a house paid in full," "old chinese cemetery  kamloops  july 1977," "the south china homecoming of klondike lee," from *Chinatown Ghosts* (Pulp Press).